The Dowager Queen.
The Hudson's Bay Company SS *Beaver*

William A. Hagelund

hancock

house

ISBN 0-88839-486-1
Copyright © 2003 William A. Hagelund

Cataloging in Publication Data
Hagelund, William A. (William Arnold), 1924–
    The dowager queen

    Includes bibliographical references and index.
    ISBN 0-88839-486-1

    1. Beaver (Steamboat) 2. Steamboats—British Columbia—
Pacific Coast History. I. Title.
VM395 B43H33 2003   387.2'044   C2001-911090-1

Editor: Nancy Miller, Yvonne Lund
Production : Bob Canlas, Ingrid Luters
Cover Design: Ingrid Luters
Front cover: Illustration of the SS *Beaver* stranded, Vancouver Maritime Museum
photo no. 3245.; design of side lever engine (mid-1800), F. DeGruchy photo.

*We acknowledge the financial support of the Government of Canada through the
Book Publishing Industry Development Program (BPIDP) for our publishing activities.*

Published simultaneously in Canada and the United States by

HANCOCK HOUSE PUBLISHERS LTD.
19313 Zero Avenue, Surrey, B.C. V3S 9R9
(604) 538-1114 Fax (604) 538-2262

HANCOCK HOUSE PUBLISHERS
1431 Harrison Avenue, Blaine, WA 98230-5005
(604) 538-1114 Fax (604) 538-2262
Web Site: www.hancockhouse.com *email:* sales@hancockhouse.com

Contents

Acknowledgments 5

Introduction 6

I Birth of a Legend (1835–1837) 10

II McNeill's Beaver (1837–1842).....................31

III *Beaver*'s Problems and the Gold Rush (1842–1862) 51

IV Navigation, Technology and the *Beaver* (1862 –1872) . . .99

V Marchant's Beaver—An Accident Waiting to Happen . . .117

Epilogue 150

Beaver Masters 158

Bibliography 159

Index 160

This book is dedicated to the memory of my
wonderful wife, Patricia Elenore, who not only
encouraged my writing, but also allowed me to
play Captain Hornblower for almost ten years
aboard the lovely replica, SS *Beaver.*

W. A. H.

Acknowledgments

For their contributions and assistance, I would like to thank the *Vancouver Sun, Province* and Victoria *Times Colonist* newspapers; *Harbour and Shipping* magazine; Captain George McInnes, for his historic notes and pictures; Dr. Robin Percival Smith for his review of chapter 2, "McNeill's *Beaver*"; and Captain D. Farina, Frank DeGruchy, Lt. Cmdr. W. E. (Dusty) Rhodes and Lt. Cmdr. Robert McIlwaine for information and pictures.

Introduction

Less than 200 years ago, trading with Natives for fur pelts was the prime pursuit of those who struggled through the wilderness of New Caledonia, a name bestowed by Simon Fraser on this rugged tortured northwest corner of America. Within a score of years after the Hudson's Bay Company ship, the *Beaver*, arrived on the Pacific coast, the glitter of gold in New Caledonia's many rivers and streams stimulated a transformation of this inhospitable region into the great country we enjoy today. The *Beaver*'s contributions played an important role in this transformation.

Through most of those historic years, while this vast domain was being discovered and developed, the splash of her paddlewheels and the screech of her whistle proudly announced her steam-age presence to every cove and inlet she visited. She encouraged the use of this new power to enhance more profitable returns from the infant logging, fishing and mining endeavors; these industries had become our prime sources of commerce by the time the more populated eastern provinces of Canada formed a confederacy of self-government.

British Columbia officially became Canada's western-most province on July 20, 1871, and only then did the country truly become a dominion from sea to sea. And to ensure it should remain ever thus, a ribbon of steel called the Canadian Pacific Railway was laid tidewater to tidewater. *Beaver* saw it all, steaming on until July, 1888, when she was wrecked at Prospect Point in Vancouver.

She remained above water at this spot for another four years, while much of her historic parts were spirited away by souvenir hunters, before slipping down into the concealing depths. While few during those desperate, far-off pioneer years had time or energy to mourn her going, many today have finally realized what an important link she actually was and have attempted to collect much of her memorabilia so those who follow may appreciate her contribution to the formation of Canada.

The Hudson's Bay Company (the oldest company in Canada) was given Royal Charter by King Charles II in 1670 to trade in furs and minerals in the area of the new world discovered by Captain Henry Hudson (Hudson's Bay named in his honor). Their traders and voyageurs dared during those earlier years to venture far afield from this area; the company was subsequently granted extensions to their trade charter because of this fact until their domain stretched west from the Red River to the waters of the Pacific Ocean and as far north as the Arctic Sea.

Such profitable growth did not go unnoticed and many other fur-trading ventures were launched, but only one grew in scope and wealth to really challenge the HBC's claim of dominion. This company had created the furry beaver as their corporate emblem. The North West Trading Company evolved from the endeavors of the French Canadian voyageurs and fur hunters who struggled west from Montreal up the rivers and lakes into Upper Canada and onto its vast prairies beyond.

A partner in this company set out to discover an overland route to reach the untapped trade area of the Pacific Northwest, after Captain Cook's ship landed a number of valuable silver otter pelts, presumably acquired there. His name was Alexander Mackenzie and his great journey created an epic chapter in Canadian history. Though he established trading posts and a route to the Pacific Ocean, neither proved profitable through the years that followed. In 1804, after absorbing the XY Trading Company, the North West Trading Company sent forth another courageous explorer named Simon Fraser to discover a more profitable route to the West Coast.

Creating trading forts along the way that were to prove profitable locations, such as Fort McLeod, Fort Fraser, Fort St. James and Fort George, Fraser discovered the mighty river that bears his name and descended down its torturous route to reach saltwater at what is today the great seaport of Vancouver. Unfortunately, this route had to await development of first a road, then a railway to become profitable, and this was many years into the future.

The third route to the coast, and the one which realized the earliest use, was that discovered by David Thompson in 1810. It reached the long inland tributaries of the mighty Columbia River by traveling much of the way southward from the Vermilion Pass, via the lakes of the Kootenay or Okanagan Valleys from the Big Bend areas. This less arduous route was used for years by the Hudson's Bay Company's great pack trains to reach Fort Vancouver on the Columbia River.

While the discovery of this route would enhance western trading for both companies, it did not realize exclusive fur trade with the Indians. American competition had already arrived on the Columbia River, before either the HBC or the North West Trading Company could establish them there. John Jacob Astor acting on advice from Captain John Mears, a pioneer sailing ship trader to the West Coast, was building Fort Astoria at the mouth of the Columbia River when David Thompson arrived there.

Ironically though, while the Americans had fought so dearly on the east coast to win their independence, the British, Spanish and Russians had already divided up the Pacific Coast so the Union Jack would fly over that portion between the California territory and the Alaskan Panhandle. John Jacob Astor, a staunch Yankee through and through, thumbed his nose at John Bull and built his fort where it commanded both sea and river traffic.

While unbearable taxation of their whaling and agricultural products by the King had angered the American colonist into revolt that realized self government in 1783, their own attempts to seize parts of Canada around the Great Lakes caused both British imperialist and settlers to take up arms and drive the Americans out of their domain. This so-called War of 1812 gave Britain the opportunity to take over Fort Astoria.

The *Isaac Todd*, armed with twenty cannons and a troop of soldiers, sailed from England carrying letters of Marquee authorizing the North West Trading Company to take over this establishment. Prudently, the Pacific Fur Company of John Jacob Astor agreed to sell their assets and vacate. By the time the HBC paddlewheel steamer *Beaver* arrived in 1836, the North West Company had been absorbed into the Hudson's Bay Company. Fort George (formerly Fort Astoria) flying the HBC flag guarded

8

this tranquil river, while aggressive growth northward was the prime pursuit of its jaunty action-packed governor, George Simpson.

The North West Trading Company had named its official seat of business in Montreal, Beaver House. It had also named one of its trading vessels *Beaver*, and, of course, the beaver adorned its coat of arms. Thus, it was fitting that on the eve of the company's absorption into the HBC, former directors of the North West (now chairing positions within the HBC) were honored by having the first steamship built for the company named *Beaver*.

This is the story of the grand old ship known as the *Beaver*. It tells how she came to be built, why she came here and the services she rendered, changing forever the country she came to serve, while in the process creating a legend that has weathered more than 150 years of telling. Fortunately, many of the pioneers to this coast were meticulous record keepers, as were the mariners and their agents. These records provide many references to the events and concerns that shaped their experiences and guided their actions. This story also leans heavily on work already published by the esteemed early writers, and credit is gratefully acknowledged of this source.

Skilled though those earlier writers were, few, if any, were mariners or engineers. As a result, often their narratives of these type of events lacked real perspective and depth to create a true understanding of the difficult obstacles the pioneers of that era surmounted in order to accomplish the simplest of projects. What this book attempts to show is the numerous impediments faced by the early pioneers and how they persevered against them, as well as how many of these events reflect an era we now know as the birth of the industrial age.

CHAPTER ONE

Birth of a Legend
[1835-1837]

ENGINEERING, IN ITS ENTIRE DIVERSE RAMIFICATION, WAS JUST beginning to be realized as the 1800s unfolded. Men who could grasp its principals and shape its potential to their needs were to become the new giants of commerce. Their creations were to become the new gods of the world.

The Hudson's Bay Company's *Beaver* was one of those gods. A brigantine rigged side-wheel paddle steamer launched in London in 1835, she arrived at Fort Vancouver on the Columbia River in the spring of 1836, and served on this coast for more than fifty years before being wrecked at Prospect Point in 1888.

Her continued successful presence here on this coast for almost twenty years before other steamships or steam-powered equipment followed her, gave *Beaver* a solitary place in everyone's imagination. She served a hostile coast and managed to set in place the circumstances that would bring industry and commerce to an area few people of that day really cared about.

The coast of British Columbia, including the areas of Cape Flattery and Alaska, presents one of the world's most rugged pieces of maritime real estate. The wind-ship sailors avoided it at all cost, and referred to it as "the graveyard of the Pacific." It was aptly nicknamed. Islands, islets, reefs, rocks and underwater sea mounts are continuously honed sharp and wicked by storms and currents, while fifteen- to twenty-five-foot tides swirl around and through these hazards. If the wind did not drive a sailing vessel onto their deadly fangs, the tidal current probably would.

The heavily timbered land mass that lay eastward of this cloud-shrouded coast was gouged with almost impossible canyons spewing out torrents of runoff waters from the frozen, snow-topped mountains that marched southward in four major ranges. While lush valleys often footed these mountains, few travelable routes traversed them. Thus, New Caledonia's remoteness from the old world, coupled with this hostile terrain, caused it to be one of the last places on earth to receive the benefits of civilization. It took the cry of gold to bring the first band of rugged pioneers into this country, and it took the dream of a railway to entice its early settlers to call it home.

Three major rivers drain this huge area, which exceeds 1,000 miles in length and 500 miles in width. The Skeena River drains the Omineca and Coast Mountains west toward Prince Rupert. The Columbia and Rocky Mountain ranges are drained southward by the mighty Columbia River, which finally arrives at the Pacific Ocean almost 2,000 miles from its headwaters, where the states of Washington and Oregon border its banks.

The third major river within British Columbia is the greatest one of all. Within this spectacular province, the Fraser River shocks its viewers with raw grandeur. It annually gouges out and transports million of tons of rock and minerals from the alluvial soils deposited millenniums ago by an ice cap that covered the entire province. The Fraser River has its headwaters in the Rocky Mountain Trench, not many miles apart from the same lake that forms the source of the south-seeking Columbia River, but drains north and westward until it reaches Prince George. There it begins a southward 2,000-foot descent toward Vancouver, picking up the large runoff from the Quesnel, Cottonwood, Bridge and Thompson Rivers, until its volume exceeds any other in the province.

Squeezing into the sheer canyons above Lillooet, it finally funnels through Hell's Gate, 100 miles southward, in an unbelievable cataract that bursts out at the town of old Fort Yale. Spreading its burden of soil westward for 100 miles from the site of old Fort Hope, it has created a lush valley area that surrounds the site of old Fort Langley, and further westward created the deltas and islands that border the Strait of Georgia.

From Fort Kamloops, where the Yellowhead Pass and the Thompson Rivers arrive, a valley stretches southward, less harsh

11

than that of the Fraser River route, and more arid than either the Columbia or Kootney routes, its waterway a mere trickle that connects a series of placid lakes to reach Fort Colville. This was the route favored by the great fur-trading caravans that traversed either the Big Bend trail after crossing the Rocky Mountain Range through the Vermilion Pass, or the course pioneered by Governor Simpson further north using the Yellowhead route from Jasper House.

The mere logistics of traveling these pioneer routes would boggle the mind of today's casual tourist driving over skyline roads that skirt the hazards of yesteryears. Caches of supplies had to be left along these routes for the return journey. Horses, canoes and equipment had to be portaged or left behind when traversing difficult section of the route. Most supplies finally arrived at the coastal trading forts on the backs of men who had walked thousands of miles to deliver it. The furs the traders had gathered had to be carried back over the same route on the same backs, along with the food and necessities of the packer's very existence.

While the Columbia River's broad waterway to the Pacific enticed the building of Fort Vancouver and Astoria (Fort George) as shipping points for ocean going ships bound for London or the Orient, this great river could often belie its placid countenance as it poured out into the Pacific. Here, weather, tides, storms and shoaling bottoms wrecked many wind ships carrying in the trade goods for the following year or those outbound with the previous year's trade of priceless furs and pelts.

Until the Dewdney Trail was pioneered to bring the traders from Fort Colville over the Coast range to Fort Langley, there seemed no way to avoid this hazardous loss of trade goods, except to lug it eastward over the Rockies to Fort Athabaska, thence by canoe and wagon to Fort Garry (Winnipeg), south of Hudson's Bay. But, even after Fort Langley and Fort Hope were connected with Fort Colville by the Dewdney Trail, the Fraser River often flooded these earlier sites and Fort Langley was moved several times to locate it above the flooding waters of this muddy river.

Fortunately, Governor Simpson had already built a saltwater trading and shipping post, which seemed to avoid all these problems. This was Fort Nisqually on Puget Sound, where the city of Tacoma now stands. A reasonable overland trail connected it with Fort Vancouver, over which trade could be hauled and both small coasting vessels and oceangoing ships could reach a sheltered deepwater dock. This ensured safer handling of both trade goods and furs.

It was for this fort that Governor Simpson requested a steamship. One which could assist or tow in sailing ships from Cape Flattery, push up the mighty Fraser to Fort Langley, or travel the length of this entire coast and transport all this trade right to the dock at Fort Nisqually. But there was another concern very real to this practical visionary, whose enterprising policies were spreading the domain of the Hudson's Bay Company across this vast wilderness.

Simpson not only had to show dominion over all he wished to hold, but he had to make it unprofitable for others who were trying to encroach on these preserves. The Russians had already seized his most northerly post on the Stikine River, and American traders were offering rum and guns to the Natives south of Fort Simpson. A powerful vessel, well armed and capable of trading within the myriads of tide and wind swept islands he argued, must be realized without delay.

The *Beaver* arrived here long before river gold drove hordes of people into the interior wilderness of New Caledonia. She came because George Simpson (knighted Sir George in 1841), governor of the northern districts of the Hudson's Bay Company, needed a special vessel to hold this wilderness empire together. He suggested the lords of the company consider a small, stout ship powered by steam raised in boilers fired with wood, of which this coast had unlimited amounts, be built and sent out with dispatch. Contrary to strong arguments from others within the company's service that thought steam a frivolous thing, his request was favorably acted upon and the next forty years proved the wisdom of this decision.

The *Beaver* was built to the highest specifications of her day at a cost of £16 per ton. She was created of English oak, African teak, elm, greenheart (hardwood from British Guiana — immune to teredos) and deal (softwood planks — i.e. pine/fir). Her hull

13

was sheathed and bolted in copper. She rose quickly on the banks of the Thames at the Blackwall Yard of Green, Wigram & Green. A standard "East Indiaman" wooden hulled sailing ship with one great exception, she was also to be powered by steam. Her hull measured 100 feet between perpendiculars with a beam of twenty feet and a depth of hold of eleven feet giving a measurement of 187 tons. Her masts and bowsprit were of red pine and her spars of Norwegian pine. She was launched as hull # 218 on May 2, 1835, and christened *Beaver* by the sister-in-law of the vice-president of the Board of Trade.

The pioneer engineering firm of Boulton and Watt supplied her engines and boilers. James Watt had created the first commercial steam engines by the turn of the century; John Boulton created the machines to build them. George Stephenson ran one of these early engines, and in 1822 created the first successful passenger-carrying railway using the broad gauge of the horse-drawn coal wagon tramway. He powered this railway with his revolutionary steam locomotive *Rocket* using Watt's engine and valve gear designs.

The *Beaver*'s engines were a pair of vertical cylinders, not unlike Watt's earlier pumping engines; but these engines had side levers, rather than an overhead beam and parallel motion, to transmit their power to the cranking shafts of the side wheels. These side levers, akin to a teeter-totter, were fitted on either side of each upright cylinder with their trunnion bearings bolted down on the engine bed so that they rocked up and down in unison with the overhead crosshead through extension rods. This in turn tugged or pushed on the paddlewheel crank axle through a massive connecting rod. Both cylinders were of thirty-six-inch diameter with a stroke of three feet and weighed almost thirty tons each developing approximately 35 horsepower.

Her boilers were placed aft of her engines, and her paddlewheels were mounted forward of her engines, thus giving her a rather strange look, even for her day, though it suited well the brigantine rig she was supplied with. Her boilers were made of iron, unlike Newcomen's atmospheric engines, which were supplied with copper boilers. The *Beaver*'s boilers consisted of rectangular wrought iron boxes connected together by wrought iron

14

tubes and suspended over a bricked furnace. They could supply steam at 2.5 psi, a feat few other boilermakers could match, but as we shall see they were subject to much trouble to accomplish this. The paddlewheels were 6½ feet wide and 13 feet in diameter, and could manage a modest 18–24 rpm with this pressure, driving the ship at 4–6 knots. This satisfied the company and they took delivery on June 15, 1835.

Launched also about the same time, was the bark *Columbia* at the London Blackwall Shipyard, she was to serve the company as a supply vessel and was made ready to sail to the West Coast, as consort to the ungainly *Beaver*, whose paddlewheels were dismantled and stowed on deck for the voyage. Both ships loading supplies for New Caledonia sailed August 31, 1835, from the Downs. Heavily laden and the weather foul and wet, the *Beaver* proved herself an able sailor and often had to shorten sail, or hove-to, to allow the *Columbia* to catch up.

Captain David Home and his crew of ten seamen appeared to have little trouble with the *Beaver*'s brigantine rig. The three square sails on the foremast were put to good use when the wind was full and by, and her fore and aft sails made working up to the weather less arduous than for her larger consort. They sighted Madeira at noon of September 13, and Trinidad on October 15. By November they were off the Falklands, and on 20 November the *Beaver* rounded Cape Horn in snow and heavy gales.

She anchored for five days at the island of Juan Fernandez, from December 13–18, to repair storm damage before heading north to the Sandwich Islands. On December 17, prior to his departure, David Home sent a message back to the London office from Juan Fernandez (the island of Robinson Crusoe) describing conditions and his estimate of his new command.

"I have much pleasure in informing you of the safe arrival of the *Beaver* at this place after a very stormy passage. I have been induced to put into this port, partly to get a fresh supply of water, as ours had become so thick it was almost impossible to drink, also to refresh the crew, who stand much in need of it, we had 4 men sick, Mssrs. Hamilton, Dodds, and myself have also been unwell, in fact, during the last 6 weeks we have not had 2 successive dry days.

"The *Beaver* is an excellent Sea Boat, and should the engines go wrong will answer as a sailing Vessel perfectly well. We lost sight of the *Columbia* in a squall near the Line, but I am happy to acquaint you with her safety also, she hove in sight 2 days after our arrival here, intending to anchor here for water, but could not get in.

"This is the most infamous place I have ever laid in, I have had to shift my berth 3 times, and have been lying with 2 Anchors down, the wind blowing from all points of the Compass and heavy gust from the shore. We hoved up with 55 fathoms of chain in 12 fathoms (depth). I therefore, thought it better for Capt. Darby (commanding *Columbia*) to remain outside, and take sufficient water aboard to supply him at sea. We have been detained here 5 days, and sail today."

The *Beaver* finally crossed the equator January 14, 1836, and on February 7 she anchored in Honolulu Harbor, departing on the February 25 to make a landfall off the Columbia River bar on March 19 after an extremely unpleasant passage. But it wasn't until April 10, 1836, that she finally dropped her anchor off Fort Vancouver eighty miles up the Columbia River (across from the present city of Portland), her long voyage safely over. She was 225 days out of London.

Fort Vancouver, established twelve years earlier on the north bank of the Columbia River, was entering its twilight years as a wilderness trading center of the Hudson's Bay Company. American settlers began to arrive out on the coast over the Oregon Trail in increasingly large numbers, driving away the game and the Indians who hunted them. Like Fort George at the river's mouth, these pioneer posts were also in jeopardy by the tempest moods of the Pacific Ocean over the Columbia's shallow bar. The creating of Fort Nisqually on Puget Sound and the arrival of the *Beaver* would, through the next score of years, sound their death knell.

Few trading posts had a more beautiful setting, nestled among gentle hills whose lush valleys ran with streams of snow-fresh water. It enjoyed a temperate climate all year round, abounded in fish, fowl and game, and in any direction stands of prime timber sighed in the balmy breezes. Stretching north and south, a few miles inland of this so-called Shangri-la, were the majestic snow-topped peaks of the Cascade Mountains.

These mountains were known as Tah-one-lat-clah—Fire Mountains in Indian legends. Early Spanish and British navigators marked their charts by their fiery plumes, later explorers named them for those pioneer recorders: Mount Shasta, McLoughlin, Jefferson, Hood, Adams, St. Helens, Rainier and Baker. The fur traders' trail to Fort Nisqually was through the Cowlitz Valley at the foot of Mount St. Helens' western slopes. Fort Vancouver lay forty miles away on its southern slopes.

Beaver's arrival coincided with a long period of Mount St. Helens activity that had commenced in August, 1831, when her eruptions had darkened the midday sun, forcing those at the fort to light candles to carry on their work. On the very day that *Beaver* was launched in London, Dr. Meredith Gardner, the HBC physician at Fort Vancouver recorded that Mount St. Helens, after three days of being shrouded in clouds of ash, exposed itself denuded of its ice-capped mantle with what appeared through the spyglass as molten lava on its southern face.

Though this was later discounted, puffs of sulfur-smelling vapors continued over the years from this mountain until late November, 1842. This violent and fiery eruption was witnessed by a Methodist missionary, J. L. Parrish and reported to the Rev. H. B. Brewer at the Dalles, who recorded it in his diary. "A vast column of lurid smoke and flame shot up until reaching a great height above the mountain, spreading out like a huge plate, below which the flames and smoke of the eruption reflected."

A French Canadian voyageur in the area reported the light at night was so bright from the eruption he could see the blades of grass at midnight near his cabin. At a Cowlitz Mission, Father Bolduc reported that on December 5, 1842, at least three craters were erupting and the Toutle River carried downstream large amounts of cinders and scoria, which killed many fish.

The Royal Ontario Museum of Archaeology in Toronto had a painting by the Canadian artist Paul Kane depicting Mount St. Helens erupting from its northwest slope, which faces the Cowlitz Valley; however, it was March of 1847 when Kane observed this eruption. In 1857 the Washington newspaper *Republican* reported that from Nisqually Plains, fire and smoke could be seen erupting from Mount St. Helens.

(During the following hundred years St. Helens lay quiet, loggers cut her timber stands, summer visitors camped on her meadowed hummocks, and hunting and fishing lodges were built for her visitors. Then in 1980 with little warning, and that unheeded by many, a gigantic section of Mount St. Helens' icy top blew off, unleashing hot gales of sulfuric gases that snapped off standing timber and spewed them like toothpicks across her eastern flanks, flooding rivers and lakes with hot ash that suffocated and buried all in its path. Now, once again silent, the new forest thickening, birds and people returning, Mount St. Helens is continuously monitored for early warning.)

Aboard the *Beaver* back in 1836, work was immediately taken in hand to refit the paddlewheels and prove out her machinery. On May 16 steam was raised and trial runs undertaken on the Columbia River. This proved such an enjoyable experience that for the next month she ran excursions up and down the river. These evoked considerable enthusiasm from the dour servants of the honorable company, though Chief Factor John McLoughlin returning to Fort Nisqually shortly thereafter voiced his skepticism in no uncertain terms. This bit of frivolous enterprise had revealed the *Beaver*'s great weakness—she burnt more wood in her furnaces in a day, than a crew of woodchoppers could chop in two days. And, the ship could barely carry more than three or four days' supply!

This was to be her bane for the next twenty or so years, until she put a crew of miners ashore at Nanaimo in 1854 to dig up coal that would increase her range of operation between fuel stops. In England, during her trial runs that had so encouraged the lords of the company, there had been a source of good coal and hard wood, and these had been mixed together to heat the brick furnace and raise steam. The soft woods that grew so prolifically from the Columbia River north through British Columbia and Alaska were heavy with resins, sap and moisture. The first two ingredients distilled copious amounts of flammable gases that required a high degree of furnace heat for ignition. But, the frequent opening of the furnace doors to toss in these quick-burning lengths of cordwood, allowed large amounts of cold air to enter the furnaces above the fires and reduce the temperature below that required for complete combustion or to drive off the moisture being vaporized from the wood.

Thus, the *Beaver* belched large clouds of gray-white smoke and sparks from her tall funnel. This, coupled with her loud wheeze of atmospheric exhaust and shower of steam, and the splashing of the strange turning paddlewheels so frightened the Indians of the area that they ran away and hid—certain that the white man had brought an evil devil into their peaceful river.

This diet of wood saps, resin and moisture had a far greater curse to the *Beaver* than frightening away the people with whom she wished to trade. It slowly deteriorated the plates and rivets of her iron boilers, and the mortar of her brick furnace. Also, as the oxides and soot built up on the thick iron surfaces, it greatly reduced the transfer of heat to the water inside the boiler—as did the deposits of salts and minerals she concentrated inside the boiler from the jet condensers saltwater entraining in her boiler feed. Much of this wasted heat being carried off in her smoke to the detriment of her rigging and spars increased her need to consume even more wood fuel.

Unable to eradicate any of these hazards, her officers put on a good front of being in full command of the situation, but Captain Home put his vessel under sail at every opportunity, so his engineer Peter Arthur could take those opportunities to clean, inspect and repair his boilers.

To more fully appreciate the problems involved in those early days of steam, and how the *Beaver* and later steamships overcame them, let's digress here for a moment. Because the earlier boilers of both Newcomen and Watt could not produce much more steam pressure than in an average electric kettle today, their engines were inefficient large affairs. The first engines utilized a horsepower cannon borer to achieve a rough cut bore in the cylinder casting, with an equally roughcast piston, lapped smooth and wrapped with jute or junk, to make it steam tight! The engineers of that day actually used the boiler steam to create a partial vacuum, and thus cause their piston to move with atmospheric pressure (14.7 psi) only. In fact, Newcomen's first pumping engine accomplished all of this within just one end of the cylinder (single-acting), relying on atmospheric pressure to force the piston up on the working stroke, and steam and gravity to force it back down again on the return stroke.

The rapid condensing of exhaust steam in Watt's double-acting engine produced greater power at the crank pin, i.e., negative pressure on one side of the piston plus positive (boiler) pressure on the opposite side by a jet of cold water spraying down through a vertical length of the exhaust pipe. But, this required a continuous supply of cold water with a pressure head sufficient to create a spray in the pipe. Not too difficult to find around a shore plant, where even a meandering stream could be dammed to create a head of water.

But at sea, it required a mechanically driven pump to create the pressure head for a jet condenser that would realize a partial vacuum to assist the steam pressure on the other side of the piston, to move the engine. Unfortunately, the only source of cooling water available to the *Beaver*, was the saltwater the vessel sailed on. When mixed with the boiler feed in this type of condenser, the water was forced back into the boiler by a second pump. Thus, it wasn't long until the *Beaver*'s boiler water was heavily contaminated with salts, which readily precipitated out as salt cake or calcium scale upon the heating surfaces inside the boiler. As much of this evaporation usually took place right over the hottest spot in the furnace, this was where the scale often settled. These areas were then more subject to overheating, erosion and possible failure.

Both the boiler feed pump and the jet condenser water pump were driven by the main engine, and in the case of the condenser water pump, this meant no condensing effect until the engine was running. Therefore, the engine had to exhaust to atmosphere through a flapper type valve that would seal tight once a negative pressure in the exhaust system was realized. Because of this, large quantities of fresh water would be lost to the atmosphere during start-up, and when fresh water was in short supply, boiler makeup water would have to be drawn from the sea.

A final note about her engines—when boilers were first put aboard wooden hulled sailing ships, they were carried much the same way that the earlier American whaling ships had fitted their try kettles for rendering oil out of blubber, on deck and bricked-in to create a furnace in which the rind of render blubber was burnt. This reduced somewhat the fearful hazards of shipboard fire, when the working movement of the ship, and the thermal stresses induced in the brick's bonding mortar, often caused cracks in the furnace walls from which smoke and flames could, and often did, escape. But, in the *Beaver*'s case, the heavy boilers and propelling machinery had to be installed down inside the wooden frame work of the hull to maintain stability in a vessel already laden aloft with a great deal of top hamper, which in itself required a clear deck for line and sail handling. While most steamships of this era, trading out of nearby European ports could carry their small supplies of coals below decks in bunkers well clear of the furnaces, the *Beaver*'s supply of wood fuel far exceeded these stowage areas, and had to be carried either on deck or share valuable hold space with her paying cargo.

The fear of fire within these wooden ships was more real to those earlier steamboat adventurers, than even a boiler failure from overheated plates. Consider these circumstances and how they must have weighed on the shoulders of the men whose job it was to make the *Beaver* a safe, reliable and viable service.

Salt in the boiler water would settle and build up on the heating surfaces allowing the iron plates of the boiler to overheat and weaken, which even with the modest pressure carried could have been sufficient to bulge the plate toward the fire. Cracking of that layer of scale above this overheated plate that had bulged could allow boiler water to squirt onto the red-hot metal, causing a flash of steam greater than the dead weight safety valves could release, and the boiler might explode. Anyone who has inadvertently lifted the lid of a boiling pot knows how quickly and how painfully the escaping steam can burn. A boiler holding a million or more times that pot of boiling water, even under the modest pressure of a few pounds per square inch as in the *Beaver*'s case, would scald most of the people within that hull to a jelly in seconds. And, keep in mind *Beaver*'s crew, all two and a half dozen of them, and any passengers had to be accommodated within the same confinement (she had no deck cabins) as this giant pressure cooker!

Conversely, if the boiler heating surfaces were coated with soot or resin from the wood fires in the furnace and could not conduct much of the heat released within the furnace into the water within the boiler, the funnel and uptakes would quickly overheat and start fires in the nearby woodwork. *Beaver*'s tall funnel was designed to not only give her good furnace draft for burning her fuel (hot air rising is called the chimney effect), but also contain the still-hot fly ash until its heat had dissipated to a safe level (below 400°F) before discharging it well clear of her spars and sails.

An even more serious fire hazard was the undetected cracks or fractures in the furnace's bricked walls that could belch out sparks and flames when the ship was working in a heavy seaway, especially if the crew's attention was directed elsewhere, thus creating the possibility of starting a fire in the ship's internals. Indeed, the *Beaver* was visited by fire on several occasions from this cause, though the watchfulness of her crew prevented most from becoming major or disrupting her schedule.

Though the *Beaver*'s hull and engines were stoutly built and withstood more than fifty years of hard work, her boilers did not. She went through five sets of boilers sent out from England before Captain Spratt's Albion Iron Works in Victoria built her a steel cylindrical return tubular type in 1877. With this boiler (now on display at Vancouver Maritime Museum) and certain other mechanical improvements, they increased her horsepower fourfold, reduced her fuel costs 50 percent and even increased her speed so she could compete with vessels years younger than herself.

On June 25, 1836, unaware of the legend she was about to create, the *Beaver* steamed down the Columbia River. She left behind young James Douglas (who would later become the first governor of British Columbia) as chief clerk at Fort Vancouver,

22

and anchored off Fort George to take aboard Duncan Finlayson, the HBC's Chief Factor in charge of northern trading posts, and John Dunn, a noted trader and interpreter. Both had traveled south from Fort Nisqually to join her.

After the War of 1812, the westward movement of Americans challenged the Hudson's Bay Company's sovereignty south of the 49th parallel, and sea borne traders from the eastern states (referred disdainfully to, as "Boston Pedlars" by HBC servants) visited the New Caledonia coast to outbid and outmaneuver the HBC traders. *Beaver*'s major role was to consistently go where these wind ship traders dared not and secure trade relations with the Indians in these remote and near untenable locations, thereby securing prime pelts at lowest prices.

Dr. McLoughlin, chief factor with the Hudson's Bay Company, held little faith that the *Beaver* could carry out this job. He had observed her gluttonous appetite for wood during his visit to Fort Vancouver. Her slow speed and large crew seemed proof to him that the company had made a terrible decision. He openly referred to her as an expensive luxury, "Simpson's Folly." He soon was given ample opportunity to deny ever suggesting it; yet, his critical candor of Governor Simpson's ideas and the HBC's changing policies was to cause him great difficulties through the years ahead.

Though Governor Simpson had considered Fort Langley earlier as a possible seaport to supersede Fort Vancouver, the terrible rapids above Fort Yale and the river's seasonal flood levels denied that being realized. All trade routes led south through the natural valleys footing the snow-capped towering Cascade, Columbia and Rocky Mountains. This, at first, appeared to make Fort Vancouver on the Columbia River a reachable destination for the voyagers and pack trains. But the disheartening toll of wind ships lost at the bar guarding the Columbia River's entrance precluded this trading post ever fulfilling its potential.

The *Beaver*'s secondary role was to provide transportation of trade stuffs and supplies between the established coastal trading forts and Fort Nisqually, which oceangoing sailing ships such as the HBC's *Columbia* could reach with less hazards and losses than experienced in entering the Columbia River.

Both Simon Fraser and Alexander Mackenzie had on their earlier trips of discovery located sites for trading posts and marked routes that led out to the sea. Dr. John McLoughlin, under the dictates of Governor Simpson had established two forts on saltwater that made transportation of people and goods between these inland trade sites and the coast possible.

Thus, in late June, with Chief Factor Duncan Finlayson and his interpreter crammed aboard the heavily laden *Beaver*, Capt. David Home crossed the Columbia River Bar and headed north into the uncharted wilds above Vancouver Island. With a crew of thirty-one including four stokers and thirteen woodchoppers, mostly Kanakas (Sandwich Islanders), she carried away her starboard paddle box off Nootka Sound. On June 27, fearing a fuel shortage, the ship was put under sail until she reached Milbanke Sound where a wood stop could be made.

Few people today can truly appreciate the staunchness of character these dedicated early explorers of the Hudson's Bay Company exemplified, as they boldly carried forth the company's business into the most hostile regions of this country's wild and foreboding domains. They were hundreds, if not thousands, of miles away from any help, often afoot over treacherous ground where a broken limb or serious infection was almost a death sentence.

While the Native Indians generally traded in good faith with the HBC—even selling their services as guides, interpreters and packers, there were those who had grown suspicious, devious and bloodthirsty from their contact with the white man. Much of this could be blamed on their earlier contact with the unscrupulous traders who swarmed out to this coast after Captain Cook's ships returned with prime mink and silver otter pelts. The outcome of these earlier unfair dealings with the Natives was their retaliation in the form of distrust and thievery, which culminated in the destroying of several trading vessels and the killing of their crews. The *Tonquin* and *Atahualpa* were recipients of this hostility.

The *Beaver*, like most of the HBC's ships, was well armed, carrying cannons, cutlasses and muskets. But being steam powered, she was not subject to the distressing calms visited upon

24

most sailing vessels that ventured onto this coast, when speed and distance were the only safeguards from an Indian attack.

It is extremely difficult for us today to realize all the hazards faced by a wind ship navigating this coast 150 years ago, or to appreciate the prudence and caution required at all times to safe guard this only bastion of succor enjoyed by the crew. Always, the ship had to be placed where she could get underway with favorable winds, or secured with anchors or ropes so as not to drift into an unattainable position when subjected to contrary conditions of tide, current or wind. Often her only salvation was to sound the depth of water around known hazards from a long-boat, before departing a safe berth. Then, more often than not, to be towed by those same longboats while they swung a hand lead ahead to prove sufficient depth of water to the next safe mooring spot. The *Beaver*, utilizing her mechanical propulsion, often could brave many of these difficult conditions, yet arrive safely at a destination unattainable to a wind ship of equal burden.

This did not save her, of course, from harassment from Natives who followed her slow progress up the coast or made angry overtures while she was at anchor with woodchoppers ashore cutting a supply of fuel. The tall rainforests grew right down to the water's edge and afforded great cover for these Indian visits, frequently timed with evening or morning darkness, or heavy fog and rain to conceal their movement. The *Beaver's* crew was constantly on the alert for such attacks, and an armed watch was kept day and night.

Indeed, Tom Johnson, a crewmember on that first trip later recalled during an interview, "We were off Kilcat when a tribe of Indians took objection to our warlike appearance, we had can-nons fore and aft, and (they) prepared to make trouble. A scout informed us of our peril, but we decided to stand our ground, so when the first band appeared on the shore, shouting and clam-bering into their canoes, we fire our forward gun. Immediately, the woods in the vicinity became alive with Siwash braves. There seemed to me to be 20,000 of them. Many swarmed around us and attempted to climb our decks. We beat them off, but had to cut our anchor chains to get away before we were boarded."

It's true the *Beaver* had the appearance of a small man-of-war with brass cannons, muskets and cutlasses in racks around the mainmast and hand grenades in safe places. This was also recorded in Dr. J. S. Helmcken's notes, a pioneer HBC physician of that time. The *Beaver* progressed on after taking in water and wood at Milbanke Sound, and stood into Fort McLoughlin (Llama Passage, across from where the Indian village of Bella Bella now stands) on June 30.

Here, young Dr. Tolmie and a fresh supply of trade goods were put ashore. A year later his diary recorded his observation of this lonely service, "Since coming here what most frequently has been a matter of cogitation, is the dullness of this place and of life in the 'Pays Sauvage' in general."

After a brief visit to the head of North Bentinck Arm (where now stands the village of Bella Coola), to view the point of Mackenzie's arrival at saltwater, the *Beaver* continued her exploratory northward journey into the unknown. On July 13 she finally arrived at the site of Fort Simpson (a day's sail north of where the present seaport of Prince Rupert now stands). This trading post, upon Governor Simpson's acceptance of some very faulty information, had first been unsuccessfully located further north. This information had been logged in 1826 by the captain of the brig *William and Ann*, stating he had proved the Nass River was navigable into the interior and enjoyed a large safe harbor well suited for a trading fort, where it emptied into the sea. Governor Simpson had ordered Chief Factor McLoughlin to build a trading fort there. But when Dr. McLoughlin realized the Nass River to be as tempest an outpouring as the Fraser and the harbor difficult to reach and prone to silting, he sent Peter Ogden north in the *Dryad* to relocate the fort at the mouth of the Stikine River. In much later years this was to become one of the famous routes up into the Klondike gold fields, which created the port of Wrangle.

Back in 1833 the Russians held claim to much of Alaska, and tolerated no encroachment of their preserves, driving the Hudson's Bay men away with a show of cannons and guns and seizing their newly constructed trading fort, even though it was ten miles outside their jurisdiction. The outcome of this bitter encounter awaited settlement through the international courts. Meanwhile, Dr. McLoughlin had Fort Simpson rebuilt further south, on the Tsimpsean peninsula.

The *Beaver* left Fort Simpson to explore the long waterways that stretch inland from this point, and discovered numerous Indian villages in the process. On her southward voyage from this outpost, the *Beaver* again visited Fort McLoughlin where some Bella Bella Indians just returning from the north end of Vancouver Island, showed them some stones that burned.

Captain Home and Duncan Finlayson had both been instructed by Dr. McLoughlin to check out stories he had heard of a source of coal, somewhere on Vancouver Island. Realizing these soft brown lumps were a form of coal, different from English black coals, and might find use as fuel for the *Beaver*'s furnaces, they sent word south to the chief factor of their intentions to sail for the area described by the Indians to locate the outcrop and test the coals.

It was at this time that the story of the first *Beaver* replica was played out. The local Bella Bella Indians had been quite smitten by this white man's creation that belched smoke and steam and threshed the water into foam as it pushed along against wind and current, and decided they too must have one. Unable to conceive the workings within the *Beaver*, they decided to duplicate at least her outward appearance and locomotion.

While the *Beaver* was away to Fort Simpson, the Natives hollowed out a huge log and rigged wooden paddlewheels, then covered this over with bent saplings upon which sealskin was stretched taunt. With a few steering and guiding paddles carefully concealed, they were able (with a dozen braves cranking the paddlewheels) to make reasonable progress. However, on the *Beaver*'s return, they realized the most important aspect was lacking—that of a tall funnel belching smoke and steam.

These Natives, who had only been exposed to white man's skills for just a few years, were not lacking in ingenuity when the desire was strong enough. With a hollow log rigged up through the cover as a funnel and dyed to look like the *Beaver*'s, they built a fire on a stone hearth within the canoe. The Indians were jubilant. Their replica belched smoke and vapor just like the

27

Hudson's Bay ship. Unfortunately, they were not as watchful of their fire as the Hudson's Bay men, and amid choking clouds of smoke both within and without, the replica burst into fire and was abandoned to drift away in a fiery pyre.

South of Malcolm Island, on Vancouver Island's northeast shores, Donald Finlayson and the *Beaver*'s boat crew spent considerable time searching for the outcrop of coals. What they finally found near the beach line amid the wind swept tall grasses and wild berry bushes was badly eroded but recognizable as lignite, a form of brown bituminous coal. Digging down a few feet produced more promising results, and a goodly sample of this was taken back to the *Beaver*. When added to the wood fuel it burned very hotly, creating a good deal of steam and only a slight brown smoke.

They rounded Cape Scott and headed south for Fort Nisqually, everyone jubilant with the *Beaver*'s performance. They had a full load of pelts, had established contact with more Indian villages then hitherto realized existed, and carried news of the coal discovery, which would improve the vessel's performance and could become a very profitable sideline in the company's large inventory of trade goods.

After reloading the *Beaver* with more trade goods and supplies at Fort Nisqually, and taking aboard a pilot for the Fraser River, Capt. Home headed north through Puget Sound, Haro and Georgia Straits for Fort Langley. In August, with favorable tides as the freshet subsided, they made the trip up river in just over three days, and the return down river in less than in one. The whole voyage took just one week!

This was a most remarkable feat, which proved without doubt the value of mechanical power over wind or muscle power under such arduous conditions. Fort Langley lay forty miles up the Fraser River, but only fifty miles below the mighty rapids and canyon which gave birth to her swift currents. Through much of the year these currents exceeded the forward motion created by the *Beaver*'s machinery, and the vessel often had to await the flooding of the saltwater tide whose influence reached this post, or be assisted upriver with shore lines or kedges, carried out by her longboats.

Westward of Fort Langley, the muddy waters of the Fraser meeting the flood tide deposited much of its burden of silt and sands within this forty-mile stretch. Over the years these materials had built a wide delta of islands and sand bars that spread the river outwards, creating many smaller waterways and reducing its great velocity to that which could be overcome by paddles and sails. It was this factor, more than anything else that determined the location chosen for Fort Langley. And, until the advent of shallow draft stern-wheeled river steamers twenty-two years later, Fort Langley, lying in the slough behind McMillan Island, was the head of navigation into this wilderness country.

The *Beaver*'s third trip from Nisqually was a visit to all the Indian villages around the Straits of Georgia, which culminated at Cowichan Bay where these fierce Natives were given a lesson in the *Beaver*'s ability to deal with unfriendly relations. Storming up against wind and tide, her funnel belching smoke and steam, her great paddles threshing the water into milky foam, she forged into the bay and with her cannons blew two large trees off the rocky point, prudently well clear of where the Natives had gathered.

Pleased with his year's service to the company, but welcome of a change away from a temperamental steamship, Captain David Home took command of the bark *Nereide*. A few years later he was lost at sea when his longboat was overwhelmed on the Columbia River Bar. Unable to cross over the storm tormented bar, the *Nereide* had stood far offshore, while David Home had the longboat crew row him ashore to make his reports and land some supplies at Fort George. He had been noted for his harsh disciplinary measures and few of his crew could recall him with fondness. He had also been strongly criticized by Chief Factor McLoughlin for his reluctance to take the *Beaver* northward through the Inside Passage. But, in all fairness, he had carried out his obligation without mishap in the face of so many difficult unknowns. The discipline he meted out was not unusual in that era, and he was certainly a worthy standard of those times, having served in the Royal Navy. The *Beaver*'s new master, though cast from a similar mold, was an American mariner out of Boston who had served more than ten years in the Pacific Coast fur trade being in command of the brig *Llama* before she was bought by the HBC.

29

Captain William H. McNeill, who after ten years service on the *Beaver* would come ashore and rise to position of chief factor in the HBC, was so admired that not only did the Indians build a totem in his likeness, but Fort Rupert, which he built, would eventually carry his name when it became Port McNeil in later years.

CHAPTER TWO

McNeill's Beaver

[1837 – 1842]

ADVISED OF THE COAL DEPOSITS FOUND ON NORTHERN VANCOUVER Island, Governor Simpson ordered that more of this coal should be gathered and sent to England to see if the returns from a market there would warrant the effort of mining, handling and shipping. In the meantime, he advised it was to be used whenever possible to fuel the Beaver's boilers, and to be stocked at the forts for heating fuel and the smithy's forge. This plan was put into practice on the first visit of the *Beaver*, in 1837, to the northern Vancouver Island area.

Unfortunately, such a tempting cargo of fuel could easily be justified to broach under the uncertain wood fuel conditions of those primitive days, and the supply of coal taken aboard up north had all but been used up by the time she came south to Fort Nisqually. On her next visit to the northern site, they dug up and loaded more coal, and then burnt a mixture of coal and wood to husband out their supply. This was more successful but still not satisfactory, so the schooner *Cadboro* accompanied her north on her third voyage, the *Beaver* towing her in and out of harbor, and she landed several hundred barrels of coal at Fort Nisqually.

The *Columbia* carried much of this coal back to London on her next voyage out, but a market for it at a price feasible to justify the effort could not be realized. The HBC decided to await a better opportunity before going into the coal business. Meanwhile, the *Beaver* took full advantage of this fuel source whenever her voyages took her near to the region, and she also shared some with the forts she visited. Though little more was done to exploit this find for the next ten years, its development in later years was to herald on stage Robert Dunsmuir, who would become known as Vancouver Island's coal baron.

Before the decision to procrastinate had become official, and while the possibility of establishing a workable coal mine in this northern area was being seriously entertained, Governor Simpson advised Dr. McLoughlin that he considered building a major trading fort in that area an ideal solution toward consolidating the company's holdings—thus utilizing to the full the *Beaver*'s potential, while allowing him to close down both Fort McLoughlin and Fort Simpson. He asked the chief factor to have the *Beaver*'s master look at this possibility on his visits to Beaver Bay, as the anchorage southwest of Haddington Island had now been designated.

The good doctor was shocked that Governor Simpson would even consider removing these two sentinels from a coast so vulnerable to infiltration by foreign sea-borne traders. Indeed, he himself would have built many more forts throughout the province if he had been given the authority to do so. He was a firm believer that to secure the country beyond any doubt, forts and trade routes had to be established. He had a great fear that the Americans, who had fought the British in two wars during the last fifty years, would quickly move northward after their westward drive against the Spanish holdings in California and annex New Caledonia from British domain.

George Simpson held much the same view as his subordinate, but felt a strong marine position, mobile and decisive, was necessary to support any system of routes and forts along the coast where days rather than months would have to realize the arrival of authority. He was also a strong advocate toward self-sufficiency. Here he had the good doctor's full support, as McLoughlin had created large farms at Fort Vancouver, Nisqually and Langley. Smoked salmon, long a staple at the forts, was supplemented with beef and pork as barnyards were built. He envisioned this as possible supply stuff to trade with those whaling ships that might visit these shores. This role did not go down well with the fur men, who scoffed at becoming farmers. So the governor arranged for retired HBC servants from the Red River Valley to move to the West Coast as overseers, and then imported Sandwich Islanders as laborers to farm these areas. Many great families living here today can trace their family roots back to these imported Hawaiian farmers.

Captain McNeill's report of the northern Vancouver Island area was a glowing one, envisioning the fort near to the coal outcrops, where good fertile ground would support farming of fresh vegetables. Low rolling hills, heavily wooded areas and good water supplies were all close at hand. Undoubtedly, it was well frequented by Indians as large mounds of clam shells and other bones were found in the area, yet the only Indians who resided anywhere near the area was the Newitty or Nahwitti, many miles to the northwest.

Fort Rupert, when it was finally built by McNeill in 1849, was a dream that never was fully realized and directed a good deal of criticism unduly onto McLoughlin shoulders because of it. Indian problems. His selection of the site of Fort Victoria had earlier leveled a great deal of criticism toward him because of its island location, and this final criticism over Fort Rupert, both projects originating from and directed by Governor Simpson, created a bitter resentment in the aging doctor who still mourned the loss of his murdered son seven years earlier at Fort Stikine, which Simpson had left unavenged.

Doctor John McLoughlin had a long and honorable service in the fur trade, rising to the rank of chief factor of Fort George in the Northwest Company, a position he ably continued under the HBC flag, until ordered in 1824 to create a large depot eighty miles upriver, where the Cowlitz Valley joined the mighty Columbia River. Fort Vancouver was envisioned as becoming the HBC western division's main supply center. Substantial buildings were erected to provide rather splendid accommodation for its officers, adequate accommodation for the workers and sturdy outbuildings and fences, for the farm animals of cows and goats plus ducks and chickens and produce storage.

The disastrous loss of ships on the Columbia River Bar during 1831–32 caused the chief factor to purchase the Bryant and Sturgis brig *Llama*, and invite Captain William McNeill and his crew into the HBC service. However, in 1833 the HBC changed its mind and built the ultimate trading and shipping port on the coast at Fort Nisqually on Puget Sound. Unfortunately, both this strategically located post and Fort Vancouver would be in American hands when the border question was finally settled.

The same year north of Vancouver Island and inside Milbank Sound, he built a smaller trading post in Llama Passage, near the Indian village of Bella Bella, which the company designated Fort McLoughlin in his honor. Before departing for London on furlough in 1843, he directed Roderick Finlayson to build a new trading fort on Vancouver Island; it would eventually replace both Fort Nisqually and Vancouver, and ultimately become capital of this far-flung land, bearing the name of the young queen who would become known worldwide as the "Mother of the Empire."

While the appointment of James Douglas as chief factor of the newly constructed Fort Victoria in 1845 would ensure Douglas's steady climb to the position of governor of the HBC in later years, he did not take up his duties there till the border crisis forced him to close down Fort Vancouver two years later. Dr. McLoughlin prudently was not as vocal over this occurrence as he had been over other policies laid down by Governor Simpson.

James Douglas enjoyed a great mentor in Governor Simpson. Born in the wilds of British Guiana on a sugar plantation, James was educated in Scotland, while his father, nicknamed "Black Douglas" took up duties as a HBC chief trader in New Caledonia. Struggling up through the prejudicial class system of those days, James Douglas followed his father into the company and found recognition for hard work and thoughtful pursuit in the eyes of Governor Simpson.

His marriage to Amelia, the half-Native daughter of Conolly the newly appointed chief factor of New Caledonia, while approved of by Simpson, was more than just frowned upon by many of the so-called landed gentry, who had themselves been shipped out to this country for being both rascals, ne'er-do-wells or worse back in the old country.

No two men appeared more opposites than Douglas and Simpson. Douglas was precise in speech, dour of countenance and meticulous in detail; Simpson was almost flamboyant, very articulate and a zealous visionary driven by purpose. But each in

34

his own particular way contributed greatly toward the creation of British Columbia. They set in place trade routes and forts that would eventually become the roads and cities which would unite this vast land into one dominion. Their contributions toward commerce, education and self-government in this rugged land, has left us the legacy of stable and peaceful development.

But this was all still in the future, as the *Beaver* sailed through 1837 under command of the former master of the brig *Llama*—a vessel which had many years of trading service in this wilderness to her credit. Captain W. H. McNeill was from Boston and was one of those terrible "Boston Pedlars" to whom Governor Simpson often referred. Simpson had solved this problem by buying the American vessel and putting both the ship and her master to work for the HBC. Captain McNeill was probably the only American to rise to high office in this honorable company of adventurers, but there were those who challenged his right to command a British ship. This became an issue when the *Beaver*'s engine room crew refused to take orders from him.

The *Beaver*'s fur book for this period shows that in early April she visited the Nass River where she traded with the Indians for 32 large beaver pelts, 13 small beaver, 20 land otter, 3 black bear skins, 152 marten, 1 fisher, 31 mink and 1 sea otter pup pelt. She then visited Seal Harbour and both Fort Simpson and Fort McLoughlin on the northern coast, before heading south to call in at the Indian villages at Nahwittie Bay, Beaver Harbour and Beaver Bay on the north end of Vancouver Island. Trading glass beads, salampore (a cotton cloth with colorful check and stripe designs), handkerchiefs, blankets, pots, pans, yards of cotton and duffel, molasses, rum, and shot and powder grossing sales of £3,500; she still suffered an overall loss of £155 to operate.

This was to be the other great bane suffered by the *Beaver*, her small size limited her carrying capacity, yet her voyages were always long and her duties many. Her fur book couldn't show this but her logbook does. Though she did not carry out naval duties as such, she was in fact the Queen's constabulary and jurisdictional arm, in this vast wilderness (Queen Victoria 1837–1901).

35

The following relates to one such incident, of which there are many.

Beaver's Log, August 24, 1837. Off Fort Simpson.
"At 2.45 p.m., the Captain came aboard, mustered the crew, carried out the stream anchor and large warp and brought her broadside to bear on the Indian village, steadied her with the kedge, cleared away the guns and got ready to fire on the Indians. The Indians returned the compliment with their musketry from the island astern. We then brought our guns to bear on them, and dislodged them with canister shot."

The *Beaver*'s trade goods were typical of that offered at most Hudson's Bay trading posts, and the rate of exchange was decidedly in the company's favor to ensure the scarcity of these goods back at the Indian villages, where their possession would enhance both the owner and the company's position. Ax heads, daggers, candle molds, both Castile and yellow soaps, buttons, needles, twine and thread, wire, fish hooks, beads, blankets and sashes were the standard trade goods available. Muskets and knives were offered as competition grew keener, and finally, against better principles, liquor was made available.

The American traders vying for this lucrative trade offered shipboard bargains, which even back in 1835 had shocked Dr. McLoughlin. He had advised London of this competition. "I watched a Boston man offer a swivil gun for a beaver, a ship's cooking Camboose or a Metal Scabbard Sabre for two Beavers. For three pelts he offered 30 gallons of molasses, or 18 gal. cask of Malaga wine, or a 100 pound cask of fine bread, or an 18 gal cask of brandy. A thirty gal. cask of rice was offered for five prime pelts. Bundles of Beaver peltries could realize four dollars American and four yards of fine calico to the Indians."

The Hudson's Bay Company had little problem inducing local Indians to work at the forts, others were content to bring in game and fish to trade, while some enticed by a feeling of prestige acted as guides or interpreters. Their fair dealings with the aboriginals, and the honor of their word with the various chiefs stood them in good stead with most of their dealings. However in every tribe there are those who do not take authority seriously, and these were the ones who often traded for spirits and to whom much of the blame must be laid for armed uprisings. The liquor provided by the fur traders had disastrous results for the Indians, causing them to hallucinate and become violent, and intimidate those who manned the lonely posts along the coast.

The lush area around Fort Rupert when it was finally built by Captain McNeill in 1847, had often been the scene of large potlatch gatherings in the past, as noted by the piles of clam shells observed by the good captain on his earlier evaluation inspection. Unlike their fierce cousins the Nootkas to the west, or the more peaceful Salish to the south, these Natives enjoyed their role as host to the great potlatches for which they became noted. After the fort was built, the Indians built a village at Su Quash, a shallow, sheltered bay less than a mile away. Often they paddled up to the fort in canoes loaded with coal from an outcrop they dug near their village. In the first year there they dug and delivered to Fort Rupert almost a thousand tons of the stuff, enjoying tobacco and other gifts in return.

Beaver often consumed much of the coals she carried from there, just to supplement the firewood she burnt to reach the next favorable safe anchorages where choppers could spend time ashore felling, sawing and splitting the huge trees. If she had been a larger vessel of greater burden, or if the coals had not burned so quickly, perhaps the coal might have found greater use as heating fuels in the forts, where green, wet firewood often created indifferent heat for the large drafty log buildings.

Though this coast appeared to offer much—its waters abounding in fish of all types, its forest offering easily worked timber while sheltering good game animals, its meadowlands and marshes overburdened with wild fruits and birds—in truth its warm, balmy days of summer were too short, while the rainy, gloomy days of the other months seemed to go on forever. This was greatly accentuated by the heavy growth of tall forests and thick, wet underbrush, making any type of travel away from the clearing around the fort's site, if not impossible, often very disagreeable. The trading rums and wines were often the only solace the HBC servants found. When consumed with a pipeful of strong tobacco by a roaring crackling wood burning fireplace, the liquor drove off the dismal solitude of this service.

Drinking was to become almost as much a problem within the trading forts, as that quickly addicting the aboriginals outside its log palisades. Though Governor Simpson, vexed by the huge supplies of both spirits and tobacco on the order books, jovially exclaimed that the HBC was its own best customer, he himself not a teetotaler did nothing to discourage it. It was left to James Douglas, in his pursuit to create settlement and industry around the trading forts, to dictate a policy of moderation and dignified deportment of all HBC servants by himself setting the example and employing only those who did likewise.

Even back in 1837, Captain Wm. McNeill had found the *Beaver*'s crew beginning to show the effects of the demon rum, and many of his rather harsh disciplinarian actions could have their cause laid at this door. Thus, he full heartedly supported the edicts of James Douglas, and these will be described further along in our story.

Returning to Nisqually by way of Johnstone Straits that first year in command of the *Beaver*, he became the first master of her to navigate through Seymour Narrows, thereby circumnavigating Vancouver Island. He expressed his pleasure with the steamship's handy response in these fast-moving tidal waters. He then made several runs with the *Beaver* through this sheltered inside passage, landing at numerous Indian villages in Knight, Loughborough and Bute Inlet, a feat Captain Homes had been reluctant to carry out. This reluctance had been criticized by both Governor Simpson and Dr. McLoughlin, and was in no small part the reason why they decided to put a more daring man in command of the *Beaver*.

In all fairness to Captain Home, he had proved the *Beaver* out through some of the most rugged waterways on the coast north of Vancouver Island, discovering much new country and extending the *Beaver*'s trade routes. The area south of this was beset with extreme tidal currents that swept through reef and rock-strewn passages around thousands of small islands and islets that could easily wreck an unknowing vessel caught at disadvantage. Captain Vancouver's account of his exploration through this area thirty years earlier under tow of his longboats, and his maps the only guide, was not easy reading for anyone viewing the great unknown. Captain Home's prudence should not be viewed as timid. The area southeast of Fort Rupert is still known today as "the jungle," and for any who have sailed through it armed with modern maps, charts and sailing direction, aboard a well-found power vessel, it is still a voyage that causes many great concern.

In the fall of 1837, Captain McNeill was requested to carry out a survey of possible harbors within the area south of Seymour Narrows that might be suitable for a major trading post in case the Americans forced the HBC out of the Columbia area. Discovering several good harbors he felt suited the future needs of the HBC, he prepared sketches of Sooke, Esquimalt and Victoria Harbors as those most readily accessible to ocean-going ships. The latter was lauded strongly in his report and echoed by James Douglas a few years later in a report to the chief factor, when conditions made it appear necessary to move the Hudson's Bay Company out of American territory.

"I am persuaded that no part of this sterile and rock bound coast will be found better adapted for the site of the proposed Depot or to combine, in a higher degree, the desired requisites, of a secure harbour accessible to shipping at every season, of good pasture, and to a certain extent, of improvable tillage lands.

"The place itself appears a perfect 'Eden' in the midst of the dreary wilderness of the north west coast, and so different is its general aspect, from the wooded, rugged regions around, that one might be pardoned for supposing it had dropped from the clouds into its present position."

Fort Adelaide was the name first proposed for this new base, but when Douglas sent back his final report after visiting the area again in 1842, it was decided to name it after the young queen, Victoria.

Even back in the fall of 1837, these things were uppermost in the governor's mind. Most important, was the apparent tentative position of the HBC at Fort Vancouver and Fort Nisqually, with the recent declaration of the 49th parallel as the border between the two countries; Americans were quickly moving into the areas of both forts. Yet, Dr. McLoughlin procrastinated for almost five years longer before sending his young factor, James Douglas north on the *Beaver* to select the exact sight in the port of Camosack and to start construction of Fort Victoria.

During those intervening five years the *Beaver* was extremely busy and many interesting events were shaping the new dominion. From Fort Garry, whence the great city of Winnipeg has grown on the Red River, westward to the Pacific Ocean and northward to the Arctic Ocean, the Hudson's Bay Company managed or policed literally thousands of people.

Their inventory of trade goods was probably the greatest in the world. Voyageurs in 100 canoe flotillas, pack trains of 200 horses, and forts containing rooms of more than 100 feet in dimension, were standard fare for this colossal company. It also boasted more than 1,000 boats or vessels, many of them deep-water sailing ships. But there was only one *Beaver*.

Governor Simpson was so in awe of her that he astounded Dr. McLoughlin after his first visit to Fort Victoria, by declaring that he was recommending to the governors of the company that all the forts on the coast, excluding Fort Simpson be closed down and that the *Beaver* be entrusted to carry out the necessary trade. While the good doctor could not believe his ears, and wondered if the governor had given leave of his senses, there was a great deal of logic behind Simpson's reasoning. But, George Simpson not bothering to explain any of this to McLoughlin, sailed the next day on a round-the-world voyage, that would touch at London, before returning to the coast in two years.

Remote on his lonely coast, Dr. McLoughlin was to remain ignorant of Simpson's intention for some time, while his worry of them was to increase almost daily. The basic cause of this concern was the realization that it was becoming more expensive each season to send out the voyageurs and pack trains to the far distant forts, while the returns in prime pelts were becoming less. There was also the disturbing change of the trend in men and women's attire. The silk top hat was replacing the beaver hat, and gas heat was replacing the need for furs in and around the home.

While the interior forts could do little about the decline of fur-bearing animals in their area, or the quality of those pelts that did come to hand, the forts on the coast had at least put an effort into other lines of exportable produces, with some degree of success. So much so that Governor Simpson, who had initiated many of them, became the favored son of the lords of the company and was nicknamed the "Little Emperor" by the jealous ones.

Here then was the logic behind all the turmoil. When fresh produce was grown at the coastal forts there was a ready market for its surplus crop, and when pigs and chickens were introduced a pathway was beaten to the forts' gates. But when the forts began drying and salting salmon, and shipping it as far away as the Sandwich Islands, the whaling fleet wintering in the shoal waters off Maalaca Bay began to visit the HBC coastal posts for supplies, and soon the HBC was shipping whale oil and bone to London.

All of this was happening while Peter Ogden spent more and more money to ship in greater quantities of goods and supplies to New Caledonia than he was sending out, while only Fort Langley and Fort Nisqually were showing a profit. Yet, small as she was, the *Beaver* carried the equivalent in cargo of at least 100 canoes or 300 packhorses as she paddled faithfully back and forth between the coastal posts, at little or no fuel cost to the company.

But the *Beaver* could do much more than this—she could tow other vessels or rafts. She could carry the company's men and business into any region of the coast, and she did it with some degree of authority when her cannons or muskets sounded. She journeyed up to the Stikine River and took over the Russian fort that was built there and sent a party up the mighty river to build Fort Taku in Alaska. The *Beaver* also carried supplies and foodstuffs to the Russians in Alaska, after a trading treaty was signed between the two companies, even towing in their ships when necessary.

She kept herself gainfully employed at all times, to the benefit of the company's image if not her profit sheet, even though much of this could not always be seen on the pages of the great ledger books. The woodchoppers of the *Beaver*, and the carpenters and workmen employed about Fort Nisqually, were not idle when neither needed their skills. Chopping down the nearby tall trees and hewing them into large deals of prime clear timber, the company shipped these back to England whenever full cargos of furs were not realized, as was the oil and baleen traded by the whaling ships putting in for fresh food supplies.

However, all was not complete harmony within this vast company. For nearly 200 years (first charter granted 1670) the wealth of prime pelts had belonged exclusively to the Hudson's Bay Company. Its supporters had recovered their investment hundreds of times over and it had created a hierarchy even more powerful than that of the East India or South Pacific Companies. The former predated the HBC by Royal decree, the latter post-dating it. The Hudson's Bay Company's chief officers were all principal stockholders in the company, its servants of clerks, factors and traders either had modest money in the company or their families did, and each had paid in coin for the position they held. Those in the pay of the company, whether ship's master, pack team master or woodchopper, signed up for a prescribed length of service in the great wilderness empire. As the encroachments by other trading nations eroded the HBC's monopoly on pelts, the heavy trapping of fur-bearing animals began to realize a depletion of stock, and the cost of labor in the field rose. Thus, the earnings of the chief officers and their servants who shared in the company's worth, decreased. This caused them to demand more of their employees and those whose role it was to supervise them, and this caused a great unrest that showed itself in people leaving the company, deserting and in some causes, in mutiny.

Indian uprisings were one thing. What the cannon could not settle, treaty and appeasement usually could. But, mutiny struck right at the heart of the great company and had to be determinedly suppressed. The Royal Navy had great experience in handling mutinies. Their peer and privilege system, their press gang crewing methods and the inhuman living conditions aboard their ships in the lower decks had made them past masters at handling human revolt. Many of the HBC shipmasters had served in the Royal Navy and, with the company demanding they run their ships in a like manner, automatically resorted to navy methods when quelling any kind of disagreement.

Captain Home had been noted for his methods while in command of the *Beaver*, but any wishful hope the crew may have had that Captain McNeill would be any different was quickly dashed within one year of his boarding the *Beaver*. Captain Home aboard the *Nereide* at Fort Vancouver, had quelled a mutiny in late 1837 by putting some of his crew in irons and meting out a dozen lashes to others. Dr. McLoughlin's report on the matter stated in part that "in the civilized world a man refusing to do his duty can be replaced by one that will, but in this country we can not easily replace him, so must make him carry out his duty, by any means available to us."

On 26 January 1838 while laying at Fort Simpson where the *Beaver* had rushed to put down an Indian uproar, two seamen alleged to have been drinking were beaten with Captain McNeill's cane for disobedience and abusive language. Two days later, two stokers suspected of the same cause were given twenty-four lashes each for disobedience. This action caused the seamen and stokers, supported by the engineers, to refuse to sail under McNeill. They only agreed to work the ship when Chief Trader John Work offered to take command. With Captain McNeill detained in his cabin as passenger, they sailed the *Beaver* back to Fort Nisqually.

Both Douglas and McLoughlin were outraged by this action, and ruled that the captain's authority must always be upheld. They reinstated McNeill to command, and put four of the *Beaver*'s crew in the stockade jail awaiting passage back to England, and had their names struck from the company's records. Harsh as this may appear, the HBC could also show compassion to those in need.

The Indians were not above ransoming any shipwrecked survivors they found to the HBC. These were often employees or servants of the company, but sometimes they were from other trading companies or even missionaries en route to bring Christianity to the Natives. Yet the HBC never once failed to do its duty to a fellow man, even when there was little hope that the recipient of their Good Samaritan deed would or could repay the debt. But the fur book also revealed a different twist when it recorded not once, but twice, that the HBC had literally purchased some Indian girls from the Nahwitti tribe. The young girls were on each occasion returned to their own tribes, from whence they had been kidnapped. The cost to the HBC was 13 red three-point blankets, 12 two-point blankets, 1 musket, 6 gallons of rum, 26 heads of tobacco, 2 tin kettles and 4 yards of salampore. Usually the Nahwitti's murdered their prisoners; these young ladies were extremely fortunate.

In late 1842 Captain McNeill, desirous of becoming a HBC factor, sailed to England aboard the *Cowlitz* to apply for British citizenship, leaving Captain William Brotchie in command of the *Beaver*. The following year Bill Brotchie was himself succeeded by Alexander Duncan, who in 1844 turned over command of the *Beaver* to Charles Humphrey. Captain Charles Dodd, formerly the *Beaver*'s second officer during her trip out from England, then took over command of the ship, a position he successfully held for the next six years before turning her over to Captain Charles E. Stuart.

This gentleman caused the *Beaver* to be seized by American authorities for infringement of revenue laws, while he himself fled by canoe back to Victoria leaving the *Beaver* at Fort Nisqually. Subsequently, unable to enter the United States again, Governor Douglas employed him at the Nanaimo coal operation which he supervised till Robert Dunsmuir arrived to take over.

Meanwhile, Captain Dodd again took over command of the *Beaver* once her differences were settled, and soon after was sailing into U.S. waters with American troops aboard to quell what began to look like a full uprising of Indian wars. During the period from 1838–43 while Fort Victoria was being planned and finally built, and while Governor Simpson was busy trying to diversify the company's interests, McLoughlin had been called back to England to give fuller account of his difficulties with the Russians, the Americans and those whose job it was to produce truck farming goods and timber. The company's view was that he had been away too long and had lost contact with their newer and larger role. The loss of exclusive trade rights in the Orient by the East India Company, and the growing feelings against the HBC's large monopoly in Canada, indicated a change in company policy was necessary.

Dr. McLoughlin's rather high-handed methods in the field and his apparent indifference to authority other than his own within the company were of great concern to the governors, who had just successfully negotiated with the British government for a twenty-year extension of their exclusive trade license in the Indian territory. Simpson's sharp rebuttal that "...he [McLoughlin] would be a radical in any country under any government and under any circumstances," was a telling blow.

McLoughlin returned to the West Coast more irate than chastened, but duly formed the Puget's Sound Agricultural Company and undertook large-scale farming around Fort Nisqually and into the Cowlitz Valley area. He also attempted to introduce farming and stock raising around Fort Kamloops and Fort Alexandria and to ship some of the goods overland to Alaska to fulfill HBC's lease agreement for their Alaskan forts. Fort Stikine alone cost the HBC 2,000 land otter skins annually, though for Taku (Fort Durham), Baron Wrangell of the Russian American Fur Company gladly accepted fresh vegetables and fruits.

The Royal Navy, after the war of 1812 with the Americans and the final spasms of the Napoleonic wars, began to take a keener interest in the Pacific. They started looking for a base for the growing fleet of warships stationed in the area. The selection of the site for Fort Victoria and the location of a large well-sheltered deepwater anchorage to the west of this port prompted the admirals to designate it their western naval base. They named it Esquimalt.

The *Beaver*'s first years of service on this coast had changed a lot of thinking both in commerce and shipping, and though many other steamships both larger and smaller than herself would shortly join her, during those earlier years her role had been both unique and exclusive. But the Royal Navy's decision to base its ships at Esquimalt and the plan of the newly formed Pacific Mail Steamships to run between Panama's overland route and the Columbia River bespoke a coming vital need for coal to fuel the new steamships.

The HBC felt it was time to offer their brown coal from northern Vancouver Island to fill this need. Captain McNeill was brought down from Fort Stikine, where he had carried out the role of chief trader, to build a fort at Beaver Bay and begin mining the known coal deposits. Scottish miners imported to carry out this latter work, resented being given a role of handyman for the fort's construction and other necessary laborer-type jobs and laid down their tools. Some even tried to desert and run away, with frightening results in this savage barbaric land. The Indians murdered several, and others perished in the wilderness.

While certain of the miner's grievances were valid, the recent discovery of gold in California and the opportunity it offered of great wealth did little to endear them to their meager HBC contract. The man who finally took charge of this mining enterprise and successfully got out the coal was Robert Dunsmuir, a Scottish miner from Ayrshire, who was also contracted to the HBC. He arrived at Fort Rupert in 1851 with his wife Joan, two young daughters and an infant son James, who had been born en route to their new home. Within the next twenty years, he would discover and develop the Wellington seams of coal and, himself, become the real coal baron of Vancouver Island.

During those early years at Fort Victoria information of more rocks that burned came to notice. An Indian from a location eighty miles north of the fort, whose nickname would become famous as "Coal Tyee," claimed his black rocks were much superior to those brown ones that were being carried down from Fort Rupert by the *Beaver*. A few months later, determined to prove this point to the Hudson's Bay men, he again appeared at the fort with his canoe half full of the stuff, and the blacksmith on trying it in his forge, claimed it was as good as any English coal. This surprise revelation echoed through the HBC just at a time when their trade was diminishing, when they had been forced to retreat northward, and the company's worth was being badly eroded by high operating costs and reduced sales of pelts.

It should be appreciated that sailing ships could seldom sail in a straight line between ports, but had to follow along the path of prevailing wind and ocean currents, and these often were quite contrary to the destination the vessels wished to reach. As a result, the sailing ship had to tack or wear a course across these wind paths, often traveling many hundreds, if not thousands, of miles out of their way to realize a landfall in an area at which they wished to arrive. Then they had to wait for a favorable wind and a convenience of weather and water current to reach a safe anchorage to deliver or pick up a cargo. While wood fuel would create steam, its fast-burning heat release and its bulky storage requirement did not lend itself to the limited carrying capacity of these necessarily small, sailing ships, which first carried steam-driven machinery as auxiliary propulsion only.

But the *Royal William* and those steamships that followed her epic voyage across 3,000 miles of the Atlantic Ocean, could travel in a direct line, which reduced traveling time and allowed the ships to be built with a reduced sailing rig to increase their carrying capacity. This allowed them to make many more profitable voyages per season. All this with neither the unreasonable wait for favorable conditions to enter a harbor nor the greater danger such dallying off a hostile lee shore might present should an onshore gale spring up.

Coal-generated steam power was the answer. Its heat release per pound was much greater than wood and its stowage much more compact. But unlike wood, which could be found on almost any coast, coal was found only in special areas where the upheavals of the earth's crust had thrust it into exposure, or weather action had exposed seams of this carbonized wood stock. Coal-fired steamships required less frequent fueling stops than wood-burning steamships, but often suitable coal supplies could not be discovered within the radius of those fuel stops; therefore, coal dumps had to be created along their routes before a service could be offered. Vancouver Island mines could, and did, supply unlimited quantities of good steam coals, thus creating a reason for steam ships to visit here and vie for cargos as they replenished their fuel bunkers.

Ironically, the new steamships that began to compete world wide for the sailing ships' cargos indirectly provided substitute revenue for those sailing ships they put out of work. Coal could be transported in wind ships unlimited distances at very reasonable cost to most fuel dumps around the world—the steamship need only run the shortest distance, coal dump to coal dump. But, it was a race of attrition; the more coal sailing ships carried to distant lands, the less premium cargos were offered to them. Within fifty years, few if any sails would dot the horizons, and steamships began to run predictable schedules.

This was the knowledge that excited the Hudson's Bay Company. If they could develop such a coal supply, the world would literally beat a path to their door. It would create industry and commerce for Vancouver Island; it would certainly generate coins for their coffers; and, most important of all, it would allow them to operate their trading business without the hazard and expense of relying on wind ships between this wilderness coast and far off England. It became one of *Beaver*'s prime requisites to locate the seams of coal, map out their areas and dig up sufficient coal to try out in her boilers and bring samples back to Victoria.

The Oregon Boundary Treaty between United States and Britain in 1846 not only fixed the boundary between their possessions at the 49th parallel, but guaranteed access to the Hudson's Bay Company into the Columbia River area and Fort Vancouver. However, misgivings still existed in the company and shortly after an Indian uprising and massacre near Walla Walla, which closed the Columbia Basin, they moved all the possessions of value from Fort Vancouver to Fort Victoria.

Not long after this, the company was given the right by parliament to develop Vancouver Island for settlement by British subjects, and the Royal Navy sent over a small man-of-war steamer to be based at Esquimalt to protect these settlers. Richard Blanshard became the first governor of Vancouver Island, and Walter Colquhoun Grant was the first landed settler.

Unfortunately, establishing new trade routes down to the coast was proving almost impossible. Portages around the Fraser River rapids proved dangerous, slow and costly; furs, horses and men slid into the river at every attempt. A route through Seton and Anderson Lakes required five changes of travel, and the Dewdney Trail crossing the Cascades from Fort Colville produced more damage than its worth. In desperation, this latter route was improved with Fort Hope as its river terminus, where canoes transferred their burden downriver to Fort Langley, while the overland trail was opened up. All this was carried out during a season of spring flooding and fall forest fires that nearly wiped out both forts.

When Chief Che-wech-i-kan, or Coal Tyee as he became known, led Joseph MacKay to the outcrops of coal at Naymo in Winthuysen Inlet, they found a large deposit of high-grade bituminous coal near the water's edge that fueled the *Beaver*'s furnace with intense heat. After the HBC was given authority to settle the island, and MacKay had carried out the initial proving of the coal deposit in Nanaimo in 1851, Governor Douglas ordered him to take possession of this area and begin mining coal.

By 1852 a small group of miners had arrived and under the direction of John Muir they created a community of log cabins, store and wharf facilities. Picking up coal from the exposed seam, they filled 480 barrels and shipped this back to Fort Victoria aboard the schooner *Cadboro*. The settlement was christened Colvilletown and the following year a bastion was built to protect the recent arrival of miners and their families.

Shortly after this they brought down Robert Dunsmuir from Fort Rupert, where he had been in charge of that operation, to put the Nanaimo workings into commercial production. A few years later, convinced that more coal was nearby, Dunsmuir formed his own company and opened a mine at Wellington. Expanding his operations to include a number of new mines and several shipping docks served by a fleet of ships and tugs to transport it, he became in the process a prince of the coal business complete with his own castle.

Events to the south would also have a great impact on the Hudson's Bay Company's tenure of this wilderness country. In 1845 the American flag was finally raised at Monterey, and the United States opened this former Spanish holding to setters. Shortly after that, rich lodes of gold were discovered in the Sierra Nevadas and the entire world stampeded to California. The gold rush of Forty Nine, and its declining years there after, left many people afoot in this vast land, most of them well bitten by the gold bug. They moved slowly but resolutely northward, following the gold-bearing sands of the rivers and streams until they stood at the Canadian border waiting for the impetus to gather before going on. The steamer *Otter* supposedly provided many with the motivation to rush northward by carrying to San Francisco a small shipment of river gold taken in trade by the HBC.

San Francisco was the growing metropolis on the West Coast. Both a pelagic and a shore-based whaling industry had sprung up with the raising of "Old Glory" on the flagpole at Monterey in 1845 and the gold rush four years later had ensured it a place in world trade. The building of the first transcontinental railway, with Southern Pacific designating this seaport as its western terminus, established San Francisco as one of the important harbors in the world. The vast trading area of the north and south Pacific Oceans could be shipped over land from this point and reach the European markets months earlier and thousand of dollars cheaper than by shipping around either the Horn of South America or the Cape of Good Hope footing Africa. And Vancouver Island held the vital fuel that both steamships and steam locomotives required to carry out this work. No wonder the officers of the HBC were excited—they could foresee much of this developing.

What no one could foresee in the mid-1850s was the impact of gold-bearing gravels on the Fraser River and its hinterland, yielding a king's ransom to those who dared fight its roaring waters and dig its rich burden. What had been an Indian territory trading in furs and other natural stuffs for white man's goods, was suddenly inundated by hundreds then thousands of gold-hungry prospectors, who cared little for the rights of either trader or Indian. Chief Factor Douglas (appointed governor of the Colony of Vancouver Island in 1851) and the *Beaver* suddenly had a policing job greater than the world, let alone the Hudson's Bay Company, had ever experienced before.

CHAPTER THREE

Beaver's Problems
and the Gold Rush
[1842 – 1862]

These previous events then were some of the occurrences that transcribed the first score of years the *Beaver* served this coast, but she had not fared as well as her dedication to duty might appear. The demands on her boiler and machinery had taken their toll, and she was sorely pressed to carry out the needs of the company. The records that still exist often refer to the difficulties experienced trying to keep the *Beaver* running. The location of such heavy pieces of machinery within a wooden hull required careful distribution of their weight upon as many frames as possible, and this was usually accomplished by fitting long heavy timbers or sleepers across the frames for much of the length of the hull's interior. This ensured the hull, composed of keel timbers, frames, keelson, strakes and planking all fastened with wooden treenails and copper bolts, would remain watertight as she twisted, sagged or stretched a little riding from wave to wave.

Unfortunately, the talent of these early wooden ship builders to accommodate heavy local loading such as steam engines and boilers would also be their swan song. For these same mechanical giants would herald in the advent of iron and steel ship construction, and the adz of the shipwright would be replaced by the steel fitter's spud wrench.

The *Beaver*'s creation best illustrates the shipwright's craft as this transition began, for she was one of the first wooden ships to be fitted with an iron heart (steam engine). The size and placement of huge pieces of wood that girthed the *Beaver*'s vital parts,

SS *Beaver*

Hull cross section **(A)** of H.B.C. *Beaver*'s contruction. Not to scale.
—W.A.H./03

1. Gunwale, 2" oak
2. Coverboard, 2" oak
3. Wale, 6" x 8" teak
4. Sheer strake, 5" oak
5. Planking, 2½" oak
6. Deck starter, 3" oak
7. 3 x 3 oak decking
8. Deck beam, 10" x 10" oak
9. Knee, 10" oak/teak
10. Sheer clamp, 5" oak
11. Ceilings, 2" oak/elm
12. Hull frame, 11" x 12" oak
13. Sister frame, 11" x 12" oak/elm/maple
14. Bilge clamp, 4" oak
15. Bilge strake, 5" greenhart
16. Futtock, 12" live oak
17. Scarfed joint C/W stop-water plugs
18. Keel, 11" x 14" oak/teak
19. Keelson, 12" x 12" oak
20. Garboard strake, 6" x 8" greenhart/oak
21. Planking, 3" oak
22. 1" fir planking overlaying tarred felt
23. 28 GA. copper sheathing over fir planks
24. Tree nail, large oak dowel, c/w hardwood wedges
25. Sister keelson/garboard clamp, 8" oak
26. Engine sleepers,10" x 16" oak
27. Ceilings, 3" oak or elm
28. Engine bed, 6" x 12" oak

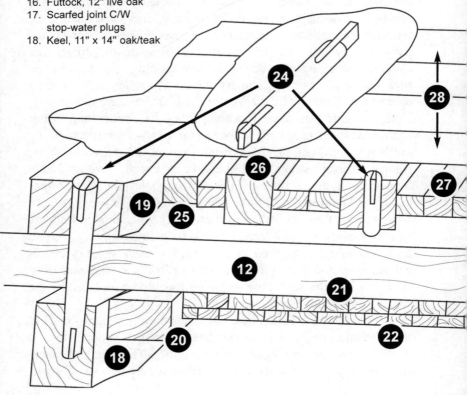

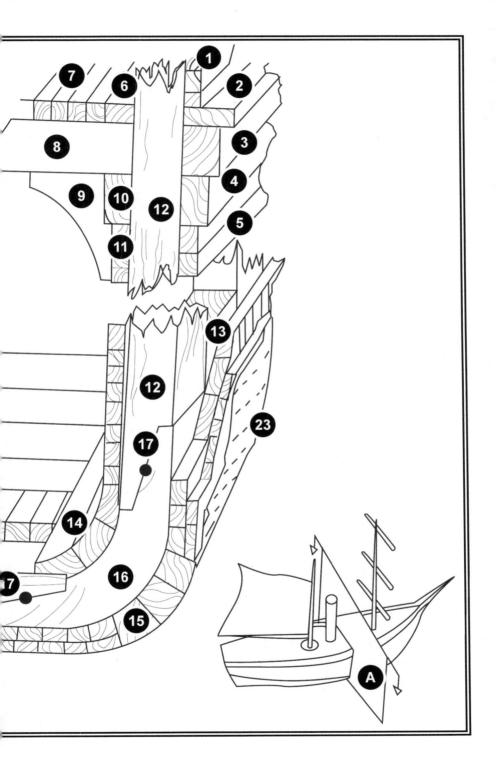

as reported in her original survey of 1835 by George Bayley, would boggle the mind of most present-day ship builders.

The *Beaver*'s main keel was of 11x14 inch elm more than 100 feet long. The keelson was of 12x12 inch African oak fastened to the keel with 1 1/8-inch iron bolts. The frames (timbers) were of English live oak 11x12 inch on 21-inch centers. Wedged in between them from keelson to waterline were oak filler timbers, which were tree nailed with an oak dowel, suitably split on the ends to receive a hardwood wedge to lock the dowel in pre-drilled hole; thus forming a solid bottom to the still unplanked hull. Upon this structure both sides of the keelson, to support the boiler and engines, were bolted four 50-foot sleepers of African oak of 10 x 16 inch sections. All of this was bolted to deck beams and floors through massive plates and straps of wrought iron.

Her planking was equally generous. The shear strakes were of 3-inch thickness and the wales at deck level above the shear strakes were of 4-inch thickness fastened with ¾-inch copper bolts. Planking of 2½-inch thickness, English elm below the water line and live oak above, was all fastened with oak tree nails or large copper rivets. Overlaying this on a bed of tarred felt was a sheathing of fir planking fastened by bronze spikes. Finally, sheets of thin copper were spiked on the hull with copper tacks to protect the ship from shipworms and toredos. This was the ship that weathered more than fifty years of heavy usage.

Pieces of machinery such as the 30-ton cylinders, the four cast iron side levers and the long, heavy 6-inch crank shaft, with 18-inch throws, carrying the 13-foot paddle wheels outboard of the hull's 20-foot beam had to have considerable clearance tolerance built into their bearing and wiping surfaces to perform useful work and not bind as the hull twisted and heaved. Such tolerances required continual lubrication and maintenance.

The *Beaver*'s heavy iron sectional boilers and the large diameter copper delivery pipes that carried the steam to the engine's throttling valves also had flexing problems that required meticulous, time-consuming repairs. The problems were due as much to mechanical stresses created by the hull as to thermal stresses created by the boiler's furnace. Heavy, stiff iron parts under torsional stresses had to rely on the bolted jointing material between each working face to allow some flexing of these parts. Yet, such movement compressed and hardened the jointing material until it could no longer seal the joint, and steam or hot water could and would blow out. Thus, this jointing material required regular attention and replacement.

The main steam pipes, which carried the steam from the boilers over to the engine's throttle valves, while constructed in soft copper were also subject to work hardening by this continual movement. They, too, had to be removed on a regular basis before becoming brittle and cracking, and then they were fire heated to a bright red color to anneal them soft again.

The boilers could not be built to flex, as each joint within these pressure vessels was of metal to metal contact. The boiler tubes relied on a hammered pinch fit and a certain degree of rusting or iron oxide buildup to remain steam tight. All plate joints in a cast-iron boiler had to rely on malleable iron rivets to hold them together. If the boiler was of cast-iron, box sectional construction, a durable bedding compound such as asbestos mixed with isinglass would be laid in between the bolt-fastened sections. The *Beaver*'s boilers had to be repaired by the laborious process of drilling and fitting copper patches or straps, or by chiseling out rivets and replacing removable sections with parts sent out from England.

While metal-working establishments of that era, located in industrial areas, enjoyed a certain degree of machine tools and the source of horse, water or steam power to operate them, the wilderness of New Caledonia, and certainly aboard the *Beaver*, offered none of these options. Drilling iron by hand was an arduous task. Carbon steel for twist drills was still in the future and chilled, iron-fluted drills had to be turned by hand while hammering or, using either a slack bow or a form of carpenter's brace, force the drill down on the work with a stout lever.

Even though a form of a strong back clamp (often referred to as an "old man") and racket drill had been invented by the 1840s, one did not reach the *Beaver*'s engineers until James Watt sent over her third boiler in the mid-1850s. Hammer and chisel remained the accepted way to fashion or repair wrought-iron fittings. Indeed, even up to the early 1900s the engineer's kit of tools always included an assortment of these tools and a bag of nuts. Rusted nuts were split open and removed, when the part was refitted new nuts coated in graphite and oil were screwed on and bumped up tight with a hammer or sledge.

But all the boilers supplied to the *Beaver* by Boulton and Watt, and she had at least four during her long career (the navy's boiler #5 appears to have been supplied by Maudslay Sons and Field of Lambeth), suffered from even a more diabolical curse. Much of their weight had to be supported by the bricked-in furnaces, even the tall funnel fitted to the top of the boiler's uptakes was supported to some extent by these bricks.

This detail, or the lack of it on the engineering drawing from Boulton and Watt, left the responsibility for bedding down the boilers in *Beaver*'s hull to the bricklayers. This was certainly so with Spratt's steel boiler (#6), the one still on display today at the Vancouver Maritime Museum. When the furnace bricks disintegrated under the waves created by the large wash from the *Yosemite*'s outbound passage in 1894, the *Beaver*'s boiler literally rolled right out of her tired old hull, carrying the port paddlewheel and sponson with it.

On the usually well-built foundations of a shore steam plant, where the weights carried by the bricks create a uniform compressive load, and thermal expansion of both the boiler and its setting can be accommodated by slip joints—such construction is quite durable and safe. In a wooden vessel that not only twists and racks to˜ the condition of seas she floats in, but heels and pitches to large angles of repose before regaining something near normal equilibrium, the brick structure carrying the heavy boilers is subjected to shearing stresses. These stresses can break or shift the brick and mortar construction. Repair of this damage must have been not only continuous, but also fraught with fire hazards in such tight cramped quarters.

Joe Carless, who had served his time with Boulton & Watt was sent out to take over as *Beaver*'s engineer from Peter Arthur in 1840, and inherited most of these problems as the *Beaver*'s boilers wearied in their last years of service. After an extensive overhaul and repairs to both the ship and her machinery, he reported her ready and able to carry out another three years of service. Much of the time Mister Carless and his second engineer had worked was spent drilling and riveting on patches. These might have been of wrought iron, for few notes on these repairs have come to light, but in all probability they were of copper. These patches and new failures in the iron fittings were a daily trial as the *Beaver* plodded up and down the coast. James Douglas, taking over much of the chief factor's duties while Dr. McLoughlin was away to England, had alerted London to this problem early in the fall of 1839 and claimed "the boilers were wearing out fast." On his return in 1840, John McLoughlin concurred and sent a letter to London. In the letter he states, "Mister Carless reports boilers possible failure at any time. New boilers should be built and sent out at the earliest convenience."

After a trip to Sitka in the fall of 1841, Mister Carless condemned the boilers as unsafe for further duty and the *Beaver* was laid up at Fort Nisqually. Bolton and Watt were again given the order to supply new boilers, and these were shipped out on the 350-ton brig Valleyfield. She had been plagued with taking in water during the whole of her outbound trip, and the cargo she landed at Fort Vancouver in July of 1842 was wet and damaged. In August she landed the new boilers at Fort Nisqually then was beached to repair a seven-foot uncaulked seam in her planking.

Mister Carless was appalled at the condition of the equipment delivered for him to install in the *Beaver*. The boilers and all their fittings were thick with rust; many of the vital joints were eroded or heavily pitted. Carless told Captain McNeill that the *Beaver* would be most fortunate if he could have her ready for duty in less than five months. This report prompted Governor Simpson to ask London if copper boilers could not be procured for this remote service. On November 15, 1843, when this second set of boilers began to show signs of failure within months of service, he wrote a further dispatch to London about the *Beaver*, which indicated a loss of confidence in his fine steamship: " ...if any repairs for machinery of *Beaver* be required hereafter, I will if necessary as you direct, get it done at Sitka. If boilers required again, it would be cheaper to send her to London, than import them.... Carless is a good engineer, but he has given notice he will retire autumn of 1844."

Less than two years later, an order was placed with Bolton and Watt for a third set of boilers for the *Beaver*. These arrived at Fort Victoria in 1847, well coated with coal tar and wrapped in cedar bark to protect them. The new boilers were bought as back-up, to prevent any loss of service when the present ones failed, but her new engineer Mister Thorne did not require them until 1849, when the *Beaver* was given a complete overhaul.

The Hudson's Bay Company's second steamer to this coast, the propeller-driven Otter, arrived from England in August, 1853. Built at Blackwall on Thames by Green, Wigrams & Green as a running mate for the sidewheeler *Beaver*, she boasted the newest in propulsion equipment. Indeed, her engines, built by Maudslay and Field of Lambeth, had been on display in London at the "Great Exhibition," and a builder's model is still on display at the London Kensington Science Museum today. For those who have the opportunity, a visit to this museum will reveal many builder models that depict the great evolution of design and construction that finally realized a stern propeller with an overhung rudder, which ultimately allowed construction of the modern steamship.

The evolution of screw propulsion had many failures, due in no small part to the construction of wooden ships' sterns and the engines then available. Problems were also due to uncertainty about what a water screw was capable of. Archimedes had invented the screw to lift water within an inclined pipe. The steam engineers of Watt's day attempted to make it propel a vessel by fastening the pump casing to the stern of a vessel, then attaching a steam engine to the impeller or screw shaft, thus, in theory at least, driving the vessel ahead by discharging the water astern. Next, they replaced the screw with a hub and fanlike blades and then removed it from the tube or casing.

They further improved this reaction-type of propulsion by reducing the large blades to a few; perhaps two, three or even four, well-built stouter blades. All had the same axial position on the hub, but were placed tangential of each other and the rudder was carried within the stream of their discharge. Thus, any deflection of the rudder would give a transverse thrust to the stern and turn the vessel.

The Otter was a bark-rigged vessel 120 feet in length with twenty-foot beams, and it displaced more than 200 tons. Her twin horizontal engines cranked a shaft that extended out through her sternpost and there connected to a liftable portion of shafting that carried the propeller. The reason for lifting this massive unit was to reduce its drag in the water while the ship was under sail. Many ingenious methods from hinged joints (universal) to folding propellers blades have been used to overcome this problem, and each has its own number of headaches to achieve this compromise.

For his Arctic explorations, Roald Amundsen's round-bottomed *Fram* had a liftable propeller, with heavy guides and a slip-joint clutch, to protect this unit while the ship was pinched in the ice. The *Otter*, pioneering a similar approach years earlier, taxed both the ingenuity and composure of her crew. Sheers legs and lifting tackle were required to be rigged out over the stern, and the whole crew were employed to carry out the maneuver. When this had to be carried out under more trying conditions, the main yard could be backed and used as a boom to rig the lifting gear. It was not a job that could be left until the last moment nor could it always be trusted.

The *Otter*'s steering rudder and her liftable stern propeller still had not learned to work harmoniously together on her arrival off Cape Flattery in early August of 1853, and caught in the strong currents off Tatoosh she nearly came to grief. By the time she reached Fort Victoria and was inspected by Governor Douglas, the engineers had carried out repairs that seemed more promising, and there is no further reference that the propeller was ever again lifted aboard.

Off loading cargo for Fort Nisqually into the schooner *Cadboro*, she then loaded cargo for "Ninimo" (original spelling of Nanaimo). On August 18th the *Otter* took aboard Governor Douglas and Colonial Surveyor J. D. Pemberton, and after returning a two-gun salute from the fort, took the schooner *Mary Dare* in tow and proceeded northward. Governor Douglas was impressed with her speed and recorded in his notes that she made the eighty-mile trip in just less than ten hours.

At Nanaimo, the governor's party was given a cannon salute by the sloop *Recovery*, before disembarking to make a thorough inspection of the coal workings. The *Otter* took aboard full bunkers of coal, before reloading her passengers and proceeding north to Cape Mudge. She averaged a good eight knots on this fuel and arrived back at Fort Victoria on August 30.

For the remainder of the year Captain Millar made trading voyages to each of the northern forts, and in December rescued Captain Parker and three crewmen from the wreck of the *Lord Weston* in Clayoquot Sound. The *Otter* had also been employed in towing the bark *Archimedes* to sea, and in hauling the small iron framed schooner *Alice* off the sands at Port Townsend. In February of 1854, the Otter made her first trip south to San Francisco with a cargo of coal and farm produce. It was a trip she would successfully make many times, before inadvertently divulging the secret of New Caledonia's gold.

Governor Douglas' policy to dry up the Hudson's Bay Company's drinking habits, on the West Coast at least, had a back lash that surfaced with the first visit of the *Otter* to the rip-roaring mining town of Frisco. The crew of this ship viewed the saloons of Frisco like parched souls, and her logbook records many instances of their over indulgence at these watering holes. Mister Thorne who had done such a noble job in keeping the *Beaver* running on her old boilers, is noted many times by the chief officer John Swanson, as too intoxicated to carry out his duty and using the most abusive language imaginable. Other members of the crew were also noted as drunk and incapacitated. The carpenter and second engineer do not escape this notoriety when it plagued Mister Swanson's efforts to work the ship. By October of that year, Mister Thorne had been put on the beach and a new chief engineer appointed to carry out his duties. Three months later it was Captain Millar who was discharged for addiction to spirits. His problem had surfaced on the voyage out from England, and had been suffered by John Swanson who had to carry out most of the work of running the ship during that two-year period. Governor Douglas assembled the ship's crew on January 8, 1855, and appointed John Swanson master of the

Otter, and this high-caliber mariner rid the ship of drunks and brought her up to first-class status.

Both Captain Swanson of the *Otter* and Captain Dodds of the *Beaver* proved themselves exceptional servants of the Hudson's Bay Company. Both had worked their way up to command after arriving out in this wilderness service for the HBC. They set a style of command that was above reproach, and this became a standard that others soon followed. They certainly complimented the fair dealing policy that James Douglas began to set in place, and which in the tumultuous next ten years would be the vital stuff which held this country together, as Aboriginals' and traders' rights were challenged on all hands by a great flood of near lawless gold seekers.

While Dr. McCloughlin had retired in 1846, James Douglas did not move his family or officially take over Fort Victoria till 1849, when Fort Vancouver was officially closed. Two years later gold was discovered in the Queen Charlotte Islands, and John Work in charge of Fort Simpson was directed to proceed there and prove out its worth. Several Hudson's Bay work parties sent over by Douglas blasted this vein of gold at Mitchell Inlet many times during the next two years.

Each occasion resulted in some rich ore being found, but on every occasion much of this ore was lost to the Natives of the area who were most hostile, first in driving away the miners, and secondly in stealing the gold bearing ores that had been blasted loose. Two fine vessels, the *Una* and *Georgiana*, were wrecked and became total losses in this effort before the Hudson's Bay Company abandoned the unprofitable venture.

The Indian affairs of these pre-gold rush years also provided James Douglas with good training for the events ahead. In 1853, after two Indians had murdered a Hudson's Bay man, Douglas boarded the *Beaver* and sailed north towing the *Recovery* and several boats from HMS *Thetis*, carrying a company of more than 130 men.

Landing at Cowichan River, he was met by a hostile group of Indians, but his calm determination finally brought reason to bear and they forfeited the member of their tribe who had carried out the murder. After he had been secured aboard the *Beaver*, the group headed north checking out the Indian villages along the way until they managed to capture the second culprit after a long chase through the woods. The *Beaver* anchored in Nanaimo Harbour where a court of inquiry was held, and the two Natives convicted. They were led to Gallows Point on Protection Island and, in the presence of the whole tribe, were duly hung there.

In 1855, the American government requested the services of the Hudson's Bay Company to put down an Indian uprising in the Washington Territory, and Douglas offered to send the *Beaver*. The *Otter* arrived from the north first, so Douglas purchased with his own funds, rifles, powder and balls from the HBC stores and sent the *Otter* to Olympia. Much of the Americans' troubles were caused by well-intended treaty agreements made with the Indians by their field officers, being abused by the settlers and not supported by the federal politicians.

James Douglas, aware of the Indians' keen sense of honor, always upheld the HBC part of any agreement with them, and always insisted they do likewise. He saw that the Natives were duly rewarded when they did and were duly punished when they did not. This relationship created a great deal of respect for the HBC, from which both the Aboriginal and the white man profited.

The terror in Washington Territory continued for several months. Finally in 1856, with thirty U.S. Army soldiers, their commander Captain Maloney and Judge Lander squeezed aboard a heavily laden *Beaver*, they faced Chief Leschi across the beach of the Steilacoom reservation. Dr. Tolmie of Fort Nisqually never let on that the *Beaver* was unarmed, but her show of authority, long appreciated by the Nisqually chief was sufficient to deter him of further terror, and he departed peaceably with his braves for their Puyallup reservation.

__ In August of this same year, the *Otter* was dispatched to Cowichan Bay after an Indian had dangerously wounded a settler named Thomas Williams. She carried more than 140 men and towed HMS *Trincolmalee* and five large boats astern manned by local militiamen. James Douglas again landed on the beach and demanded the Natives give up the culprit. When one of the Indians raised a gun and attempted to shoot the governor, the other members of the tribe were so impressed by the governor's resolute stance, that when the gun misfired they quickly seized the man and turned him over to the governor. Douglas immediately convened a court, where the Native was given a fair hearing. Finding him guilty, Douglas ordered him hung right on the spot. Needless to say, this fierce tribe of Indians, who like the Haidas of the Charlottes were the terror of the coast, took this lesson to heart and created few further acts of murder.

In 1856, a large group of miners who had discovered gold in the gravels of the Pend d'Oreille River near Fort Colville during the autumn, surged across the border and forged up the Columbia River. By July, 1857, these miners reached the Thompson River and were realizing £2 to £8 a day in gold dust and flakes. Others following the rush into Fort Colville elected to go over land on the Dewdney Trail and try the Fraser River gravels. Their results were even more spectacular, and it was supposedly 1,400 ounces of the gold bought by the Hudson's Bay at Fort Kamloops and Fort Hope that the Otter carried to San Francisco.

The American government in appreciation of the Hudson's Bay assistance in her recent Indian War, offered to install a more permanent type shaft and propeller in the *Otter* at their Mare Island Navy base, and also to remove much of her top hamper and fit more cabin accommodation on deck. The *Otter*'s gold was delivered to the Navy to pay for these repairs.

By the time she was again ready to sail north, some of the miners from the Fraser and Thompson Rivers who had returned to Frisco with a modest poke of gold, enhanced their experiences with wild tales of even greater strikes being found by those who had decided to winter in the north. When these tales were augmented by the story of the *Otter*'s gold, it created a stir of excitement in the unemployed prospectors of this waning mining city.

The *Otter* was quickly followed north by the much larger Pacific Mail's steam sidewheeler *Commodore*, which landed 450 miners at Fort Victoria on Sunday morning, April 25, 1858— awakening this small staid populace, in no uncertain terms, to its new role as staging and supply center for the gold fields. Unfortunately, the *Otter* had already sailed to Fort Langley and the *Beaver* was away servicing the north coast forts, when this wild bunch of flannel-shirted, back-packing, armed men deposited their mining gear on the beach.

Many of the newcomers were British or American (thirty-six of whom were African-American) and the rest were German, French or Italian. All wanted transportation to the Fraser River. Within a short time, many, too impatient to wait for the HBC ships to return, set off to leap frog through the Gulf Islands, using canoes, small boats or rafts to make the short water passages that separated these convenient stepping stones. Drenched by chilling rains and hazarded by storms, currents and debris in the river after reaching the mainland, many died. Those who succeeded in reaching Fort Langley, quickly gained the gold-bearing river bars a mile south of Fort Hope and worked their way toward Fort Yale.

Sensing a new El Dorado in the making, the idle steamships in San Francisco offered passage to Fort Victoria at $30 a head and, carrying three times their normal capacity, dumped their disgruntled passengers onto the crowded beach at Victoria. By June, more than 10,000 miners had found their way onto Hill's and Emory Creek bars. Before 1858 came to an end, the number had reached nearly 25,000! Supplies for this huge influx of people had to be ferried across to the mainland then moved up the river to the forts. It was a monstrous problem of logistics that kept both the *Beaver* and *Otter* busy all that year.

Within six weeks of the first arrival of miners at Fort Victoria, 225 buildings, most crude storerooms of rough-sawn lumber or log construction had been built, and fifty-six jobbers and importers were open for business. By July, almost a million dollars of supplies had been shipped into the gold fields. San Francisco's and Victoria's merchants gloated over the trade, and when town lots in Victoria jumped from $50 to more than $3,000 a lot, late arrivals gladly paid the price to get even a meager foothold in this highly lucrative market.

The township that sprang up around the fort enjoyed a unique position—it was the only legal entry port into the vast wilderness controlled by the Hudson's Bay Company, one that James Douglas guarded with diligence fearing an American takeover. British rule and an exclusive trading right allowed him to exclude

64

Model of the SS *Beaver*, 1836
era, on view at the Vancouver
Maritime Museum.
Photo: Vancouver Maritime Museum

Copy of the 1834 contract
between the Hudson's Bay
Company (HBC) and Green,
Wigrams & Green of London to
build the 187-ton *Beaver*.
Photo: Vancouver Maritime Museum

Above left: Sir James Douglas
Photo: Vancouver Maritime Museum

Above: Dr. John McLoughlin, a chief factor with the HBC. A mountain south of Fort Vancouver was named in his honor.
Photo: Vancouver Maritime Museum

Left: Captain Charles Dodd, a *Beaver* master who had twenty-five years of HBC service. He was the 2nd officer on the maiden voyage of the ship. Dodd Narrows in Nanaimo is named after him.
Photo: Vancouver Maritime Museum

Captain John Swanson, *Beaver* master.
Photo: Vancouver Maritime Museum

Left: Captain William H. McNeill, a *Beaver* master and HBC factor.

Photo: Vancouver Maritime Museum

Below left: Captain John Sangster, *Beaver* master.

Photo: Vancouver Maritime Museum

Below right: Captain George Rudlin, *Beaver* master.

Photo: Vancouver Maritime Museum

Captain J. D. Warren, *Beaver* master.
Photo: Vancouver Maritime Museum

Captain William A. Mouat,
Beaver master.
Photo: Vancouver Maritime Museum

Above left: Robert Paterson Rithet, one of Victoria's successful entrepreneurs and owner of the *Beaver*.
Photo: Vancouver Maritime Museum

Above: Captain George Marchant, last master of the *Beaver*.
Photo: Vancouver Maritime Museum

Left: Edgar Crow-Baker, last owner of the *Beaver*.
Photo: Vancouver Maritime Museum

Beaver Steamer anchored in Victoria Harbour

Friday March 26th 1852   **128**

P.M. Moderate Westerly wind and Squally, with thick snow and sleet at times. three woodsellers onshore cutting fuel, two cutting saw helves remainder of the crew Employed cleaning ship and otherwise variously, Needale, Pait Settle &c At 4 P.M. a party of men belonging to the Fort went over to the village on the opposite side of the Harbour with two Boats, for the purpose of taken in custody an Indian, who had killed one Cow and a Calf yesterday, belonging to McAuley immediately after the Boat touched the beach abreast of the village the Indians took possession of her, forcing the men out of her into the other Boat, which was afloat they immediately returned to the Fort, and Shortly after maned our Harbour Boat and the Cadboro boat and proceeded over to the village well armed to demand the Prisoner Who, the Indians still refused to deliver up at 4.30 lit the fires and weighed anchor and towed the Vessel abreast of the village for the purpose of firing upon it if necessary at 4.45 anchored and Moored the Vessel and Prepared for action, at 6 the Indians Delivered the Boat back and came to an arrangement with the Governor, at 8 let the fires out and let the Vessel lay for the night &c Latter part light variable breeze from the westward and fine pleasant weather.

William Kitham Mick

Copy of logbook entry March 26, 1852. The steamer _Beaver_ is anchored in Victoria Harbour.

Photo: Vancouver Maritime Museum

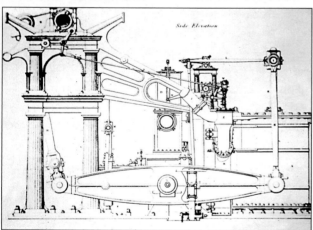

Side Elevation

Above, right and opposite:
Typical designs and installations of
side lever engine to the mid-1800s.
Photos: F. DeGruchy

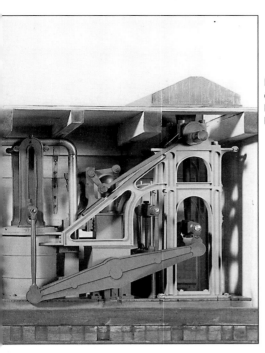

Left: Working model of the *Beaver*'s engine. Boiler design is not known. Model is on display at Vancouver Maritime Museum.

Photo: Vancouver Maritime Museum

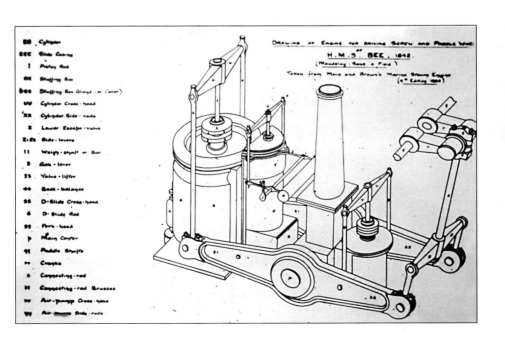

The *Beaver*'s final boiler on display near Fort Nisqually, Washington, 1909. Note the tube stoppers visible below the anchor; there are eight in total. The paddlewheel shaft is beside the boiler shell. Also note the vertical steam drum that carried the funnel.

Photo: Vancouver Maritime Museum

This is the only known picture of the *Beaver* pulled out of the water, Victoria, 1874.

Photo: Vancouver Maritime Museum

Beaver as towboat/freighter in 1882 at Quadra Island. She is seen here without masts and bowsprit. Note the galley smoke pipe from the port paddlewheel and the large top house.

Photo: Vancouver Maritime Museum

Enlargement of picture showing crewmembers. Captain Marchant is in the wheelhouse; chief engineer David Symons is in the center by the funnel.
Photo: Vancouver Maritime Museum

The *Beaver* in March, 1888, five months before her total loss.
Photo: Vancouver Maritime Museum

The *Beaver* in 1890, her second year as a wreck in First Narrows. Copper sheathing is visible below the anchor.

Photo: Vancouver Maritime Museum

This picture is from 1892. The Empress of Japan is outbound behind her. Note the funnel is supported on the steam drum.

Photo: Vancouver Maritime Museum

This picture is also from 1892. Notice that the mast has been removed—it later became a flag pole at the Burrard Yacht Club. A navigation light was mounted two years later above the *Beaver*'s stern.

Photo: Vancouver Maritime Museum

The interior of the *Beaver* in 1902. The wheelhouse and mast are in the foreground above engine frames and paddlewheel shafts. In the background is the boiler and beyond is the stern of the vessel. Notice the size of the beams, frames and planking—all oak!

Photo: Vancouver Maritime Museum

A picture of the *Beaver*'s "First Voyage of Discovery" in 1966. *Photo: F. DeGruchy*

Left: Prospect Point, before 1906. Note the new lighthouse erected above the rocks upon which the *Beaver* came to grief. The north side of the First Narrows has two dolphins indicating Calamity Reef. All that can be seen of the *Beaver* in this picture is part of her boiler and funnel.
Photo: Vancouver Maritime Museum

Lookout duty on "First Voyage of Discovery," 1966.   *Photo: F. DeGruchy*

March 30, 1995, SS *Beaver* returns to Victoria with a royal welcome. Author is standing in wheelhouse doorway. *Photo: Victoria* Times Colonist

Preparing to become SS *Beaver*, RCN, Esquimalt, B.C., 1964.
Photo: F. DeGruchy

Northward bound up Indian Arm. Raccoon Island is off the starboard bow.
Photo: D. Christie

Summer pleasures on the deck in Indian Arm.

Photo: D. Christie

Author hamming it up on the "Toys for Children Cruise" as Captain Henry Hudson of the HBC.

Photo: D. Christie

85

Company postcard of the SS *Beaver*, with insert of author dressed up as Captain Henry Hudson.

Photo: F. DeGruchy

Above right: SS *Beaver* hauled out at Vancouver shipyard, 1989.

Photo: F. DeGruchy

Right: SS *Beaver* on display at her Expo 86 berth. *Photo: Author*

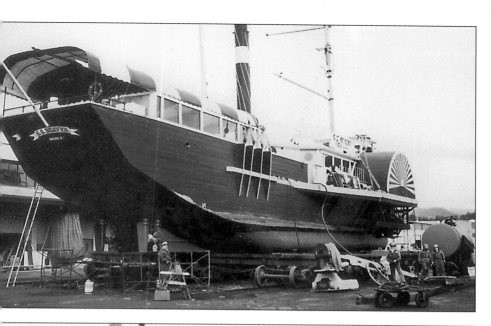

Outward bound under the Lion's Gate Bridge.

Photo: D. Christie

any ship, even a British one, from entering the waters or rivers leading into these prime preserves. And his enactment of a law to charge a royalty on exportable products, including gold, and the requirement that all miners/prospectors register for a provisional license at a charge of a guinea a month, ensured he held onto that control.

Victoria was not the only seaport to feel the excitement and trade of the gold rush, the lumber towns of Port Townsend and Whatcom (Bellingham) witnessed mass exodus of mill workers, soldiers and sailors who hacked a trail through to Fort Langley. More gold seekers arriving from San Francisco aboard steamers that bypassed Victoria, to land their passengers on American shores in Puget Sound, quickly followed them. These people plus those arriving via the interior routes overland accounted for the greater number of active miners in the Fraser River area.

The *Beaver*, arriving from her northern trading routes in late May, was astonished to find the foreshore covered with rough buildings, tents, mountains of supplies and a milling crowd of would-be gold seekers anxiously awaiting transportation up the Fraser River. Loading as many as they dared aboard, she followed the *Otter* as far as the spring freshet allowed, then off-loaded her eager passengers and their wildly assorted freight on the steep northern bank. This created the beginning of a settlement that would become known as the "Royal City." Within months it was registered as the city of New Westminster, capital of the province of British Columbia, and terminus for most steamboats plying the Fraser River. Many of the eager prospectors began working the sands as they made their way along the north bank, and numerous of these had actually reached the rich gold-bearing bars near Fort Hope, before the others who landing at Fort Langley had clambered over the trail used by the HBC pack trains.

Thus began the rush for New Caledonia's gold. A surge of humanity such as the world had never seen. They sailed, paddled and waded onto the lower bars of the Fraser River above Fort Langley, from the sea. They struggled up the Columbia and Kootenay Rivers into the Fort Steele area, which a few years later would become the first base west of Regina of the North West

Mounted Police, forerunner of the modern-day Royal Canadian Mounted Police. And they clambered over the Dewdney trail into Fort Hope from Fort Colville and the United States.

The Hudson's Bay Company, under James Douglas' untiring efforts, tried to police the entry and activities of these gold seekers, even to the point of issuing mining licenses and registering all gold sales. But for every licensed prospector busy digging up gold, there were at least a dozen or two more who had come in the back door and recognized no authority but their own. The two routes up the Fraser River became known as the Dewdney Trunk and the Yale Road, coming together near Emory Creek Bar—the richest gold-bearing bar in the Fraser River.

North of this area was the tiny post of Fort Yale and the torrent of Hell's Gate, which deterred the timid and defied the bravest. When James Douglas received reports back from this outpost, of the hundreds of miners gathering there and their lawless activities, he immediately made a trip over and assessed the situation with his own eyes. By that time the hundreds had exceeded thousands, and more were arriving each day. He requested the Royal Navy to guard the waterways and river into the area and ordered all the southern forts to register those who came through and purchased supplies. He then sent a special dispatch to England requesting authority, supplies and men to police the area. This request fell upon deaf ears. Prime Minister Gladstone and his government were more concerned with European events, and they treated this as another bit of local hysteria such as the Crimea war had created, with the proximity of Russian Alaska a few miles from Fort Simpson. England's eyes were elsewhere. The best that Secretary of State for the Colonies Sir Edward Bulwer Lytton could do was send over a young barrister, Matthew Baillie Begbie, as judge, and appoint Chartres Brew as inspector of police.

One thing Governor Douglas' visit to the gold fields had shown was the need for transportation into this wilderness area, and James Douglas wasted no time entering into an agreement with Pacific Mail Steamships to supply it. They sent the side-wheel steamers *Surprise* and *Sea Bird* north. The *Surprise* reached Fort Hope on June 6 and the *Sea Bird* later the same month, only to be lost on her return trip downriver. She was replaced by the big sternwheeler *Umatilla* from the Columbia River, which reached Fort Yale on July 16.

To ensure the Americans did not exploit this exclusive transportation opportunity, Douglas placed both the *Otter* and *Beaver* on the run across from Victoria to the Fraser. The *Umatilla* also explored a possible route up the Harrison River, and onto the head of the lake, where Port Douglas was later built. In August she retraced her route to the head of Harrison Lake, carrying 260 miners who had offered their services as construction workers, to build a road through to Lillooet. These were men unable to work the river bars due to high water from the late freshet, and who were anxious to reach the upper reaches of the Fraser. Each miner deposited $25 in the governor's fund to pay the cost of the work, and their effort in slashing out a trail ensured them the right to work the upper river, once the route bypassing the terrors of the canyon and Hell's Gate was completed. It proved a good investment for both.

The project was under command of A. C. Anderson (for whom Anderson Lake was named) and was completed by mid-October. A difficult route at best, suitable only for pack animals, it cost the Hudson's Bay Company £14,000 to realize; however, it did open another way into the upper Fraser River for both supplier and miner alike.

Douglas again visited the diggings above Fort Hope in early fall after a report was received that the Indians were trying to drive away the miners and violence had begun to brew. He arrived at Fort Yale to find the more practical miners had formed themselves into a semimilitary unit, taken some punitive action with the more belligerent miners and entered into treaty agreement with the Indians that allowed them to coexist peaceably. The miners had even built a goal of sorts at Fort Yale to house an American who had killed a miner over a claim dispute. Governor Douglas decided he must show that British justice and authority had to be upheld, and formed a court to convict the man and deport him out of the country.

While Governor Douglas of the Colony of Vancouver Island tried to carry out intentions he felt assured continued British rule of New Caledonia, as governor of the Hudson's Bay Company with exclusive Aboriginal trade in New Caledonia, he felt a strong administrative responsibility toward the inroads of this burgeon population swarming up his rivers. It took correspondence with London four months of travel, in addition to delays in debating before any decision reached him. Thus, with the swift events demanding swift action, Douglas often took it upon himself to arrive at a solution amenable to all.

Realizing the mining claim sizes were causing a problem, he had them adjusted to fit the terrain, and he delegated this matter into the hands of an appointed gold commissioner. With winter fast approaching and sufficient stock piles of supplies arriving at the mine fields to allow the miners to winter on the river, he had town sites laid out at Fort Yale and Fort Hope. The small lots were offered to the miners on which to build their winter cabins at a reasonable monthly rent, which could be applied to the purchase price, should they wish to remain in the area. While this delighted the miners, and they tried to show their appreciation by undertaking to rebuild the old brigade trail north from Fort Yale to Spuzzum, which Douglas had indicated was necessary to travel beyond Hell's Gate, his actions caused some concern in both the British parliament and the Colonial Office, who thought the Hudson's Bay Company, rather than the British government, were making profit from this recently discovered resource that had not been included nor intended by their charter.

On October 30, 1858, the *Beaver* arrived back in Victoria to witness the launching of the *Governor Douglas*, the first steamship built in New Caledonia. She was also the first British sternwheeler to ply these waters, and she took a full load of freight and passengers up to Emery Bar above Fort Hope. Douglas arrived back at Fort Victoria in time to receive the young British barrister who had traveled across United States and sailed up from San Francisco. The governor was not impressed. He had expected at the very least several experienced government servants, letters of authority and a detachment of British soldiers to maintain law and order. The tall rawboned man, who presented himself as judge-elect to the territory of New Caledonia, was both inexperienced and ignorant of maintaining law and order in a savage wilderness. "A mere child in the woods," Douglas grunted to George Pearks, the crown solicitor for Vancouver Island, before retiring to read the dispatches carried from England by Matthew Baillie Begbie. How wrong he was in this first impression, was to please him greatly during the tumultuous years ahead as the hordes of miners and suppliers reached the Cariboo to create Richfield, then later Barkerville.

Judge Matthew Baillie Begbie was to become a living legend of British justice as he rode horseback through this vast wilderness, holding court and administering justice with swift stern deliberation that earned him the unflattering title of "the Hanging Judge." Begbie, who had been well trained in British law, serving many years under the great lawyers of his day but unable to progress further while they held office, eagerly accepted this wilderness duty as a way to realize his place in law. His most famous quotation was thundered at a horde of rough belligerent miners who had taken the law into their own hands to settle a dispute. "In this land, the Queen's rule shall reign, and British justice shall prevail!"

The dispatches Douglas perused confirmed tentative plans and agreements he and Lytton had been formulating over the past seven months, and a royal proclamation had been drafted for immediate enactment. James Douglas called together the company of Hudson's Bay men and announced his resignation as chief factor of the HBC. Then as governor of the Colony of Vancouver Island he ordered a number of officials and members-elect to accompany him to Fort Langley. HMS *Satellite* delivered them to the *Otter* and *Beaver* off Point Roberts, then at old Fort Langley they all boarded the veteran *Beaver* to land at the new Fort Langley.

On November 19, 1858, under bleak skies and chilling wind, with a bright new Union Jack whipping over the main entrance of the fort, Governor Douglas read Begbie's commission as chief justice of the Colony of British Columbia. Then in the presence of the hundred people who assembled, Chief Justice Matthew Baillie Begbie read Her Majesty's commission appointing James Douglas, governor of the Colony of British Columbia. Douglas then took office and read three proclamations: the first, revoking

HBC exclusive trade on the mainland; the second, indemnifying the above and its officers of any previous acts; and third, extending British civil and criminal law to British Columbia.

The events that followed over the next five years in the gold fields, were the most exciting ever recorded, and established the economical growth that realized this colony as a valued province, in the creation of a sea-to-sea dominion. Moving northward from the Thompson River and up the muddy Fraser, the miners converged in the area that would become forever famous as the Cariboo. North of Quesnel Lake, which actually threw gold up on its wave-swept beaches, the mining town of Likely sprung up, before the surge of gold seekers swept by into Quesnel Forks, and up the Cariboo River to Keithly Creek. Here they separated, some going northwest up Keithly Creek, thus discovering the rich gold of Van Winkle and Jack of Clubs Creeks, the others going northeast to discover Grouse and Antler Creeks. The mining town of Richfield then became the gold center of the Cariboo, and here Judge Begbie held some of his most famous court cases.

But on Williams Creek in 1862, the greatest gold find of all was to establish this area as the new gold center—the true El Dorado of British Columbia. Here, Bill Barker sunk his famous fifty-four-foot shaft, ridiculed by those who rushed helter skelter over the whimsical gravels of snow-melt creeks, and came up with gravels that yielded the unbelievable returns of $1,000 a pan! Silenced was the ridicule as others rushed to dig down to these golden pay streaks.

By the end of that year Williams Creek had produced almost $3,000,000 in gold! Gold in those days enjoyed the heady price of $12 a Troy ounce. That works out to about 250,000 ounces of gold or 125 tons, but there was much more gold then which had not been accounted for. The town site of Barkerville mushroomed up above the diggings and could soon boast of being the biggest and richest city west of the Rockies and north of "Frisco."

These returns sustained a rapid growth in transportation, and transportation required establishment of trade and storage centers. Victoria had grown into a shantytown with Jewish merchants, Chinese tailors and launderers, Kanaka laborers and Negro porters. Fort Langley, which the HBC assumed would become the mainland capital and trading center, quickly laid out a settlement called Derby to compliment it, but were disappointed when Colonel Moody of the Royal Engineers selected the popular landing stage on the north bank of the Fraser, west of Fort Langley for that site. He located a camp for his army nearby it, today known as Sapperton (army engineers were known as sappers thus it was their town). In 1860, with cartage of supplies into the gold fields costing $825 a ton and taxed with a twelve-shilling per ton duty, the Yale Trail up the Canyon's precipitous sides was improved by the Royal engineers to a pack trail and later to a twelve-foot wagon road.

Because much of the gold was being sold right at the diggings to American merchants and sent directly south to San Francisco, Douglas established a gold commissioner at New Westminster and an armed escort service to ensure much of the gold arrived there. Still, much of it was spirited out of the country, tax free and unaccounted for. Thus, the true worth of these gold fields will never be known. In later years, the Chinese who flocked here to work the old gravels were believed to have shipped unrecorded amounts of gold, platinum and gemstones back to China in the coffins of Chinese being returned to their motherland for burial.

With the *Beaver* and *Otter* almost fully occupied in the transporting business to the Fraser River, the arrival of the *LaBouchere* at Esquimalt January 30, 1859, under command of Captain John F. Trivett, who formerly commanded the HBC bark *Princess Royal*, was a welcome relief. She immediately took over the northern forts and trading routes of the *Beaver*. She was almost twice the length and tonnage of the *Beaver*.

A paddlewheeler, boasting side lever engines of 180 horsepower, she was capable of ten knots and sported two funnels and ten cannons. This ship, under command of the former master of the *Otter*, John Swanson, and with Captain Dodd, former master of the *Beaver*, in charge of trading, made several successful trading trips to the far north, returning from one with the scalp of Colonel I. N. Ebey who had been murdered by the Tlingit Indians of Kupreanof Island.

In 1862, while trading at Hoonah village about 150 miles north of the Stikine River, the captain and trader were seized by about 150 Natives who had swarmed aboard after a disagreement. The chief officer armed the crew and ordered two cannons loaded with grapeshot aimed at the surging crowd. This brought a parley into play, and finally for the gift of two revolvers, the two hostages were released. Trading resumed and soon after dark the *LaBouchere* slipped her cables and sailed swiftly away.

The Stikine gold rush saw her kept busy in the north for several more years, but overall she had proved a rather expensive vessel for such work. Soon after that she was given a full overhaul and put in the more lucrative San Francisco-Victoria trade, which offered a more direct route to England. Under command of Captain W. A. Mouat, and carrying eighty-five passengers and fourteen crewmen, she struck a reef off Cape Reyes on the foggy night of April 14, 1866. Extracting herself from this pounding punishment, she steamed south toward the safety of San Francisco, on a course that kept her close inshore, but raising water levels in the boiler and engine room finally caused her to put most of her passengers in the lifeboats and send them ashore. Finally the drama came to an end, as the *LaBouchere* unable to steam any further settled deeper into the sea. Captain Mouat and those crewmembers still aboard were taken off by a fishing smack that had stood by just before this fine large steamer went down by the head.

The *Beaver*, however, still had many important events to attend before she retired. The Hudson's Bay Company operated a farm on the San Juan Islands. When they landed 1,300 sheep and a number of pigs on the islands, I. N. Ebey, the American collector of customs for Puget Sound who would later be murdered by Tlingit Indians, demanded custom dues must be paid. Governor Douglas arrived there with the Victoria collector of customs aboard the *Otter* to protest such an affront, and ordered Captain James Sangster to raise the British flag to show his authority.

While they awaited the decision of the Boundary Commission, newly arrived American settler Mr. Lyman Cutler shot and ate one of these pigs, then refused to make restitution to the HBC. The *Beaver* was again dispatched there, bristling with indignation and armament, as was the American military, and only cooler heads saved the two countries from going to war. This exciting event in June, 1859, became a celebrated affair known as the "Pig War."

The following year the *Beaver* underwent her first major refit, her rig was reduced and she was fitted with a large deck-house to increase her passenger accommodation before being placed in the Victoria to New Westminster run. The *Beaver* really had little passenger space, the few cabins in her sterncastle area were for her officers and traders; the equally tiny forecastle forward was packed by her rather large crew of woodcutters and stokers and the sailors who manned the ship. Passengers as such often found themselves forced to find rest upon the cargo in the hold, and spending their leisure exposed to the elements of her open decks. Long journeys on the *Beaver* were often recalled more because of these harsh conditions than her speediness of travel.

Refitted with passenger accommodation, she competed with the newly formed British Columbia and Victoria Steam Navigation company operating the *Governor Douglas*, and an American steamboat company operating the former Columbia River sternwheeler *Julia Barclay* for the river trade, and cut substantially into their lucrative profits. The outcome of this shipping war saw the *Julia Barclay*, outrun by the *Beaver*, retreat to the Columbia River while the *Beaver* herself, after HBC accepted $1000 a month from the B.C. & Victoria Company, was taken out of service.

HBC could now afford to lay her up at Victoria and use her as a floating warehouse and powder magazine, for they had the small steamer Caledonia and, in 1862, the large sidewheel steamer *Enterprise* to assist the *Otter* on the Fraser River run. Why they did not put her back in the northern trade has never come to light. The agreement with B.C. & Victoria Company did not include the *Otter*, thus she carried on with this service until bought up by Captain Irving's Canadian Pacific Navigation Company.

Captain Richards of the Royal Navy parleyed with Governor Douglas to charter the laid-up *Beaver* and place her into the hydrographical service, carrying on the chart-making work he had pioneered with the HMS *Hecate* and *Plumper*. For a sum of £4,000 per annum, the *Beaver* traded her Hudson's Bay Company flag for the Navy's White Ensign. HMS *Grappler* towed her over to Esquimalt for a complete overhaul while she awaited surveying equipment from England. An extended deckhouse to suit the needs of the mapmakers enclosed her decks and a boxlike wheelhouse to navigate her was built atop this cabin. Fitted with numerous small surveying boats and with a crew of twenty-nine seamen, one marine, a surgeon, hydrographer and engineer, she was place under command of Lt. Daniel Pender and sailed for Nanaimo and Fort Rupert in June, 1863.

CHAPTER FOUR

Navigation, Technology and the *Beaver*
[1862 – 1872]

HMS *BEAVER*'S ROLE AS A HYDROGRAPHICAL VESSEL WAS OFTEN interrupted to carry out other naval duties, and sometimes even civil engineering and policing duties. After checking out the upper island settlements and surveying the harbors of Fort Rupert and Nanaimo, *Beaver* was dispatched to upper Texada Island to survey the limestone deposits there with a view to opening a quarry. The following year she sailed north to chart the waters of Nekwilta Inlet, sheltering in Safety Cove while she charted Fitzhugh Channel and Queen Charlotte Sound. During this period in 1864 James Douglas retired as the colony's first governor and was knighted Sir James by Queen Victoria and elevated to the rank of Knight Commander of the Bath.

Charting the outline of a coastline, complete with elevation above and below a datum point, and soundings of the surrounding water's depth is a very exacting skill requiring all field measurements be laid out on a master-plotting plan in a especially reliable manner. Thus, the exact area that the plot covers must first be correlated to its geographical position. When Captain Vancouver carried out his observations in 1794, by using the first fully compensate clock to fix his position in Observatory Inlet north of the present-day port of Prince Rupert, he fixed this spot on his maps in relationship with Greenwich Observatory in England. From this point all the other datum points on this coast could be related. With much of this vast unknown area a blank on a sheet of paper etched with the appropriate lines of longitude and latitude, as arrived at from Captain Vancouver's position point, celestial observations could determine a cartographic position within its boundaries. This position was usually taken from a high point, easily visible from many points of the compass, and became the datum point for all other measurements. Thus, this tiny point could be fixed with some certainty on the blank sheet of paper using the grid lines of latitude and longitude to locate it. From this point all other information about the area being charted could be related and drawn in, and this would include the local variation of the magnetic compass. These field drawings could be transferred and overlaid on the master plan sheet, thereby filling in one more blank area of our coast and giving it substance, which a surveyor or navigator could use to plot a relative position.

Before delving further into the *Beaver*'s charting of the coast, it would be practical to have a quick lesson in navigation and mapping of the earth. Because the planet is a sphere, one must realize that drawing any part of its surface on a flat piece of paper will destroy the faithfulness of the projected image. Another important factor to keep in mind is that the lines of longitude converge closer together the further you travel north or south of the equator—the area between two meridians of longitude will be less the further north or south one travels. Yet, when they are laid out on a chart, the lines appear parallel. The distance between these lines obviously is in error, but when picked out in degrees, minutes and seconds of an arc they are quite reliable for the navigator's use. While a distance should not be measured across the bottom or top of a Mercator-projected navigating chart (which is created by imaging the earth's spherical surface onto a cylindrical surface), the scale created along either side (up and down) of this copied chart is accurate for the area it covers, and is divided into nautical miles and cables, as well as degrees, minutes and seconds for use in that way.

Before leaving this subject of dividing up the earth's surfaces into zones bounded by lines of latitude and longitude, one should appreciate how they came to be laid out the way they are. There is nothing mythical or predestined about them—they are merely hypothetical and appear nowhere else than on a chart or map to give boundary to the information offered there. Upon the earth's surface, man has built monuments to depict where they would be if of a physical nature, rather than of a hypothetical one, i.e., Greenwich, England, is zero (0) longitude.

The spherical shape of the earth has been known for thousands of years, if we consider the artifacts existing today that would have depicted it to those who studied such phenomena through the ages. The rotation of the earth and its annual orbit of the sun, gave man an instrument to not only deduce its shape but its size, and with this information know the distance to Cathay east or west of their position in Europe.

Another characteristic about earth that affects everything we do is the inclination of its axis and hence its surface toward the sun—cold during winter, hot during summer in the northern hemisphere, the opposite in the southern hemisphere. It did not take great leaps of science to recognize the four seasons, but it did take an astute mind to realize that twice each cycle of four seasons, the sun passed directly overhead on the same spot somewhere on earth. Now this was revolutionary! It meant at that moment the center of the sun was directly over the center of the earth, and that by finding more points east and west of this point, a circle could be projected around the earth that represented equal halves of the sphere, or zero latitude north and south.

Any other circle projected around the globe whose center touches this circle's center, was a great circle as well. Thus, by erecting a second circle whose center touched the center of the first circle around the earth, so that their circumferences crossed at ninety degrees to each other, a way to divide up the earth's surface was realized. A third circle whose center was ninety degrees to the second circle, would create points of contact with each other at top and bottom of the sphere, or North and South poles of planet earth. Parallels of latitude, nine of them at ten degrees apart above and below the zero parallel (the equator) were added, as were meridians of longitude at ten-degree increments along the periphery of the equator. The result was a grid system upon the surface of planet earth, more or less ten degrees square at the equator, becoming progressively narrower as it reached toward the poles.

Following is how a mariner arrives at a measurement. Time is measured in hours, minutes and seconds; distance is measured in degrees, minutes and seconds. To find the diameter of the earth, one must first measure its circumference, thus. Mark off the distance the sun moves across the earth's surface at the equator, say in one minute (remember 2piR = circumference). Then multiply that distance times sixty, then again by twenty-four to find the distance around the world. If we divide that distance by 360 (degrees in a circle), we learn the distance of one degree of longitude and can use this information to locate ourselves, in relation to a known geographical position. To learn the diameter of the earth at that point of latitude, divide the circumference by pi (3.1514).

Naturally, being ball shaped, the further north or south one is from the equator (zero degrees) the smaller that diameter will be. It all appears pretty simple up to this point, right? Well, maybe not that simple, but logical.

Here is where the plot gets a bit blurry. Because we created a time system (sidereal) that is based on the same celestial phenomenon, we can convert its scale of hours, minutes and seconds into degrees, minutes and seconds. Now as time and distance in this analogy can be considered the same thing, and a couple paragraphs back we ponder how long would the strip of earth be that the sun shone on in a minute of time—let us see what a little arithmetic will uncover. The earth takes twenty-three hours and fifty-six minutes to make one revolution on its axis, so fudge a bit, and call it twenty-four hours. During that 24-hour revolution we at home passed by 360 degrees, had they been plunked in the ground like a picket fence (1 degree per picket). So we could say we passed (360/24) or fifteen degrees every hour. Now there is sixty minutes in each of those hours, so by dividing minutes by degrees, i.e., 60/15, we find out it took exactly four minutes for a whole degree of distance to pass by. Get the idea? Now, there are sixty minutes of distance to each degree; so, there must be (60 divided by 4) fifteen minutes of distance that passed by for each minutes of time. Now, for want of a simple test, dig a deep hole in the ground exactly where we said we found the equator, then to the west of it, lets say a mile away, for the sun is moving deceitfully fast, dig an identical hole. Time the interval from the instant the sun's rays shine fully down to the bottom of first hole, till it does the same thing down the second hole. This time should convert to the same distance laid out between the two holes, which of course are a mile (6,080 feet) or 3.473 seconds (15 divided by 4) of time. Computed from that, the earth must have an equatorial circumference of (the number of seconds in a minute divided by the number of seconds the sun took from one hole to the next) x (the number of minutes in an hour) x (the number of hours in a day). Thus, the earth's circumference is 60 divided by 3.473 x 60 x 24 = 24,877.6 miles (officially it is 24,894 miles). Pretty smart, eh.

Now, a nautical mile is measured in cables and fathoms; a statute mile is measured in yards, feet and/or inches. The latter is the distance of a straight line from two points exactly one nautical mile apart, the former is the slightly longer track following the curvature of the earth using the same two points, i.e., 5280 feet compared to 6080 feet. A nautical mile is divided into ten equal parts called cables, disregarding those few extra feet, say 600 feet long. This makes it very handy for sound echoes (i.e., sound travels at 1,200 feet per second), thus a one second echo must have traveled out one cable (600 ft.) to the echo board, and another cable (600 ft.) back to reach your ear in one second. A fathom is one-hundredth of a cable, i.e., six feet, and a knot is a rate of speed (i.e., one nautical mile per hour) ten nautical miles per hour equals ten knots. Now back to chart making on the coast.

While Captain Mears, Barkley and Dixon had charted the areas around Nootka Sound, Barkley Sound and Dixon Entrance, and the Spaniards Galiano and Valdez charted parts of the Straits of Juan de Fuca and Georgia, these all had to be correlated onto a master plan with more precise data to locate them. Most early navigators had some means to locate their latitude through the sighting and elevations of certain stars (such as Polaris—the North Star); thus, they could sail their ships east or west by maintaining this elevation on either a chip on a string, their cross-staff, astrolabe or later the sextant.

Direction could be held fairly constant by using a compass, which very early during the exploration of the new world had replaced the lodestone. But time was the only true measure of a mariner's travel along any east-west course. His apparent travel might be calculated by his speed (using a chip log) multiplied by his hours of travel (still used today with modern instruments to calculate a dead-reckoned position). By knowing the time difference between his apparent noon (when the sun was in its zenith overhead) and when it was thus at his point of departure, or at a position such as Greenwich on longitude zero, he could calculate the distance he was from either of those location, and fix that on his globe or chart.

This was where an accurate timepiece was so valued. The sundial or sandglass was subject to many errors and useful only for short voyages between known positions. It was only when a properly compensated watch or clock could be provided to the navigator, could he truly know the time difference between his position and his point of departure or his point of reference, such as Greenwich, England. Thus, by establishing the first timed position on the Pacific Coast in Observatory Inlet (as close as he could get to the same latitude as Greenwich), Captain Vancouver created a local reference point from which to relate all other plots.

Captain Richards using HMS *Plumper* and *Hecate*, and assisted by Daniel Pender, had done much general layout on a plot of this coast. Now Lt. Pender with *Beaver* and her crew were to pinpoint even greater detail into this plot, and even discover many unknown waterways and islands hitherto unrealized. How this was carried out is of possible interest to the reader and will be described briefly and simply.

While navigators far out of sight of landmarks plotted a position on the featureless oceans to fix their ship's location, usually related to the time of sighting a known heavenly body by the use of triangulation and compass direction, the surveyors on the solidness of land had many other methods to compliment such computations. Thus, during this same period as Richards and Pender struggled to map our coast, Everest was struggling to complete a measured northerly line through India from which all other measurements could be taken. Using this line as a base, the distance off to markers, such as mountains or other known elevated features, could be found through triangulation by sighting it from the line at ninety and forty-five degrees. In such instances, the length of the other side would be equal to the length of the measured base. With this measurement, an elevation could be found using a sextant with an artificial horizon to provide the angle of the hypotenuse, and when multiplied by the ratio of this angle the length of the other side of the triangle could be found. Lt. Pender, using measured lines away from his datum point, like spokes of a wheel, could carry out the same function to locate distant features such as hill or mountaintops and even islands. Using a datum point, which had been overlaid with a brightly marked pole tower highly visible by those doing the surveying and sounding, of a known height and location above the mean high water line of that area, all field information was plotted on work pads that indicated magnetic bearing and distances from this point.

A good sextant can be used not only as a height gauge to find the length of the side of a right-angle triangle where the height of the base is known, but much like a station pointer, to give accurate horizontal angles between one or more markers in front of the observer. A properly compensated compass will give for a local area a fairly accurate bearing off a known sighted location. When local deviation is applied to this bearing it will relate fairly accurately to more distance plotted locations out of sight of the observer.

Two other methods were common at Pender's time to locate an observer's position from the datum point, but only the former required a compass. The rod and chain give highly accurate linear measurement, which might be substituted by a rope or wire over water, though both are subject to some degree of error from stretch and shrink. The other position finding method is to locate the observer through bearings in transit, that is to sight two objects in a line with one's eye, like a gun sight, only in this case it could be mountaintops or points of land. With certainty a line drawn through these objects on a plot, would also be drawn through one's position. By taking a compass bearing off fixed objects nearly at right angles, or by using a second set of bearings in transit, one's first position line can be crossed by the second

105

bearing line to fix one's location, without need of any measurements or calculations.

Over the land a surveyor sights through a transit, which has a high-power telescope complete with level and cross hairs, capable of sighting a vertical marker in relation to its own elevation and to pivot this telescope over a division plate fixed to a tripod stand, allowing the horizontal angle between the sighted position and the datum position to be read. Later the surveyor can transfer these measurements to the master plotting sheet, establishing lines of sightings or contours of elevation. Over the water, this procedure becomes a little more risky. A boat is seldom still, the water level is continually changing, and only the sighting point ashore remains fixed.

Up until present times, we had little if any idea of what really lay beneath the surface of any body of water. Any information we had was found by sounding the depth with a weighted line, and sampling the bottom by whatever stuck onto the weight and was lifted back up to the surface. For depths of twenty-five fathoms (180 feet) or less, a hand line of durable rope with markers at each six-foot interval, fitted with a ten-pound lead weight having a hollow on its lower end into which a sticky substance such as grease or tallow is bedded, will pick up a sample of the type of material on the bottom and give a reasonable measurement of the depth. For greater depths than this a windlass-type machine carries long lengths of flexible sounding wire and much heavier weight to ensure a fast descent that will not be deflected too greatly by the currents.

In gathering information about those land masses under the water, and most important those land masses that rise close enough to the surface to hazard a ship's safe passage over them, a line of soundings are made away from the shore-based datum point, noting the direction and distance off for each sounding. When these are plotted onto the master work sheet, a pattern of the contour of the land elevations below the water can be arrived at. Thus, above the water, land masses have contour lines joining like elevation that relate to known datum points and geological abnormalities. Underwater depths have sounding contours that relate to a known level of mean low-water datum point. Where sudden rises of the bottom indicate reefs or rock pinnacles that might be missed in the vertical plunging of a lead line in a row of soundings, the area can be swept with a cable towed out between two boats. When such objects warrant the effort, further soundings and bearing of the known hazard will be taken, and added to the plot.

Many of the place names given to this coast during the surveys carried out from the *Plumper, Hecate* and finally the *Beaver* by both Captains Richards and Pender, commemorated the Hudson's Bay Company people who had contributed much of their lives to its development. Being Royal Navy officers they also commemorated many of the great naval victories by using either the event or commanders' names as place names. Thus, Douglas Channel commemorates Sir James Douglas and Amelia Island, his wife Lady Douglas. Home Bay, Princess Royal Island, is named for Captain David Home, original master of the *Beaver*. McKay Point, Newcastle Island, is named after Joseph W. McKay, HBC chief trader and first legislative member of the assembly of the Colony of Vancouver Island. Helen Point, Active Pass, is for Joseph McKay's wife. McLoughlin Point, Victoria, is for Chief Trader Dr. John McLoughlin. McNeill Island, Victoria, is named after Captain William Henry McNeill, second master of the *Beaver* and later chief factor, HBC. Hood Point, Bowen Island, is after Admiral Sir Alexander Hood. Howe Sound is named for Lord Howe, hero of the naval battle known as the "Glorious First of June." Queen Charlotte Channel, Howe Sound, is after Lord Howe's famous flagship, HMS *Queen Charlotte*. Bowen Island, Howe Sound, is named after Admiral Bowen, master of HMS *Queen Charlotte*.

On the *Beaver*'s return to the south to carry out boiler repairs, Governor Seymour, who had taken over from James Douglas, requested her services to reexamine the mouth of the Fraser River. With the increased traffic into this low-lying estuary, many vessels were being stranded on these shifting sands and some even storm damaged before they could be refloated. Lieutenant Pender recommended the placement of buoys and beacons to mark the safe channels—a role still carried out today, even though the main channel is protected with a rock breakwater and annually dredged.

The *Beaver* then rushed off with HMS *Tribune* and *Sutlej* to quell a possible Indian uprising in Bentinck Arm. She was also employed that same year as supply ship to HMS *Grappler* patrolling the troubled waters of Bute Inlet, and she concluded 1864 by surveying Desolation Sound. In 1865, *Beaver* surveyed the waters of Johnstone and Broughton Straits and named a new inlet Seymour Inlet after the new governor. Then she acted as policeman by returning the body of murderer Antoine and his boat to the Nanaimo authorities

In 1866 she surveyed many of the channels around the islands north of Vancouver Island, up to 54°40" north latitude, including Skidegate Channel in the Queen Charlottes. She then acted as an examination vessel for marine pilots. Lieutenant Pender was authorized to test many local mariners' knowledge of the waters around Esquimalt, Victoria, Nanaimo and Comox and certify those whom he felt were trustworthy enough to guide in foreign ships. With the information gathered from these knowing men, many more uncharted rocks and reefs were noted on the current charts and many were named for the men who had found and identified them. Thus, Dodd Narrows, south of Nanaimo was named after Captain Charles Dodd, longtime master of the *Beaver* in the HBC service. Marchant Rock, Estevan Point (on the western coast of Vancouver Island, the only spot in Canada to suffer enemy fire since the war of 1812), was named after Captain George Marchant, last master of the *Beaver*, who discovered it in 1869.

After a late fall trip to Bella Bella, the *Beaver* went into Victoria for repairs to some hull damage she had experienced in a grounding off the Race in which several huge rocks were embedded in her hull and which remained there until she was pulled out of the water and they could be prized out. At this time she was also reboiled, and these boilers, according to her inspection certificate (the first instances ever found), were two square boilers 10 feet long built of 5/8" wrought iron plate and installed in the *Beaver* in 1867 with a test pressure of 19 psi and a working pressure allowed of 12 psi. This is really the first technical description of the *Beaver*'s boilers, though earlier reports referred to flues in her boiler, sometimes the plural "boilers" was used, and twice the term return tubular was used, no drawing had been uncovered and the above created a certain confusion.

Fortunately, curator Leonard McCann of the Vancouver Maritime Museum, on a visit to the Birmingham Public Libraries in England, found a boiler drawing from Bolton and Watt dated London, May 23, 1866, that is titled "HBC steamer *Beaver*." These show an inclined set of cast-iron header boxes approximately 2 sq. ft., into which 56 cast-iron tubes, 2 ¾-inch in diameter and 5'8" long are fitted. There are two of these units enclosed by what appears to be a cast-iron wrapper suitably bricked with refractor material through the furnace area, and two such complete boilers each 6 ft. wide, 8 ft. long and 10 ft. high are fitted into the *Beaver* with 60-in. width coal boxes on either side. It is stated that this comprises 1,159 square feet of heating surface, with a grate area of 58 sq. ft. Though more than thirty years separate the original installation and these boilers, and undoubtedly great improvements in construction techniques and iron materials had been realized, the basic design appears to fit those described in the earlier records.

Relaunched from the ways where she had been dragged out for winter repairs, the *Beaver* came to grief by sliding off into the mud, and had to be towed into deep water by HMS *Forward*. Soon after this she sailed for Fort Simpson to resume her northern surveys, and the following year surveyed much of Vancouver Harbour and English Bay—a port she would come to know intimately through the years ahead. In 1870, after charting the waters of the Straits of Juan de Fuca, Peddlers and Bechers Bay, she was decommissioned and returned to the Hudson's Bay Company.

Governor Seymour saw little future value in the ship for the HBC, and on recommendations from Chief Factor James Grahame and Captain Herbert Lewis she was put up for sale. During this time, or perhaps four years earlier when she had been laid up as a floating warehouse, James Douglas had arranged for her bell to be lent to the first public school to open in Victoria. Whether it was Norfolk or some other school is not known at the time of writing, but the original bell of the *Beaver* has not surfaced since. No school in Victoria has record of ever receiving such a bell, though several bells have claimed this distinction. Her last owner, Mr. Saunders, did fit a bell to the *Beaver* but this was from a former Chinese junk; there was another bell, very damaged, that did come from the *Beaver* but was a smaller edition, such as a hand bell.

At any rate, with or without her bell, she didn't appear to interest anyone and in 1874, when no buyer had come forward, the *Beaver* was put on the auction block, where surprisingly she realized $15,000. Even using an exchange of $5/£ sterling, this modest sum returned her original £3,000 hull investment back to the HBC. For a forty-year-old steamship, which no one had wanted a short time before, it was a surprisingly fine offer. The reason for her possible sudden worth will be explored in the next chapter.

Before following her role into private enterprise, it is important to better understand not only the events ahead, but also those events that had shaped her destiny to this point. The *Beaver*, on this coast at least, had brought a power source that had not been seen or experienced before. In a wet, rugged country where the labor of straining men or beasts supplied the only power to hew, move or build things, the *Beaver*'s effortless moving machinery fired the imagination of all entrepreneurs.

True, the horsepower (a horse-driven capstan that could be geared to drive a pinion shaft) or the waterwheel, which had ground and milled grains, pumped water and even sawn wood, had been used for years. Both these items had very limited power, were extremely fragile, were subject to wear, and were fixed to an area where feed or water supply was available. The *Beaver*'s engines were made of iron, a material just coming of age that was produced in both cottage and industrial facilities, and withstood the rigors of power applications far better than either wood or bronze.

Wrought iron was first created years before recorded history in small bloomeries (refractory lined pits) charged with iron ores (oxides), charcoal and limestone. The temperature attained was sufficient to cause the oxygen in the oxides to combine with the carbon of the charcoal to create carbon monoxide gas. The limestone combined with the impurities to create a slag which could be removed, and the pure iron left as a spongy mass in the furnace, could be worked by a smithy by hammering and folding into very ductile, strong forgings for tools or weapons. But this knowledge was not generally known, and the production of wrought iron so limited that few items created with it were traded.

Cast iron was generally realized through many of the trading countries around the fourteenth century, with an improved furnace design that allowed much higher temperatures to be realized. This very liquid state of iron allowed it to be poured into sand molds and cast into many useful shapes from iron spoons to mammoth cannons. But this metal was extremely brittle, its crystalline structure yielding low tensile strength, about a third of that of wrought iron; yet, it provided compressive strength almost double that of wrought iron. When cast iron was heated by burning charcoal in a furnace called a finery, while a supply of air passed over it, it was converted into wrought iron. Production of this wrought iron was in very limited supply until 1784, when Henry Cort created a puddling furnace where pig iron (small cast ingots of pure iron) could be heated with the hot gases from burning coal. Joseph Hall improved this furnace in 1816 by lining his furnace with iron oxides. In the early 1820s James Rastic added a waste heat boiler to the furnace, thus providing steam to operate a forging hammer for shaping the wrought iron produced. This iron provided James Watt and other engineers with a much more strong and plentiful (thus cheaper) material for engine and boiler building.

Steel was created by removing more of the carbon from iron to elongate its fiber structure; this was accomplished by blowing air through the molten iron, but its production was very limited and its quality very poor. When in 1861 Sir Henry Bessemer perfected his converter, he started steel making on a commercial basis, supplying vast quantities to industries at an affordable price, giving birth to the "age of steel." This was the miracle metal of the future, it has carried us from the pioneer days of steam into the jet age. Combined with steam it dug the coal to fire our retorts, it drilled the minerals that abounded in British

111

Columbia, and it made the rails on which to run our trains that carried these products to the marketplace.

But, such wonderful industrial progress gave little solace to the horde of argonauts seeking the whimsical traces of glinting gold, in freezing rivers or mountain canyon. The prospectors who had hewed the trees and dug the roads into the Cariboo to discover and exploit that area's golden harvest, had quickly moved further northward in search of more virgin deposits when the Cariboo's rich returns dwindled. In doing so, they opened up areas like McDame and Telegraph Creek in the Dease Lake area and stumbled onto the golden creeks of Atlin Lake and the Yukon River, which even to day continue to produce small fortunes in placer gold.

They left behind them roads, settlements and mine workings, some still producing good returns and others just ghosts of their former selves. The iron, tin, copper, lead and silver deposits they had ignored in their frantic haste for gold, lay waiting for development. When steel tools and steam power became available, wiser more practical minds turned these minerals into profits.

Coal was dug and stockpiled along new shipping routes, to enable large steamships to compete with the smaller sailing vessels. Sawmills turned the forests into lumber and timber, and ships arrived in increasing number to carry it to world markets. Trees of more than 200 feet in height produced timber clear of any knots or branches for more than 150 feet, to the amazement of foreign buyers. The production of cheap steel and tin created the ignoble tin can, a sealed container that would carry our bountiful sea harvest of salmon, herring and cod to every corner of the world in prime condition.

Steam power, especially as improvements in boilers were realized, had many wonderful uses and any surplus steam could be used for heating or processing. The vital ingredients required to realize it were found in this part of the world in prodigious amounts. Water rushed off the mountains in torrents, wood grew on the mountains in forests that boggled the eye, and fat oily fish and whales abounded in the waters that lapped these mountains. It was left only to the ingenuity of man to create the tools that could harvest the bounties of this country as marketable goods, and steam was the power that he harnessed to perform this work.

Those years that spanned this great period of development set in place the equipment and skills that would cause even greater leaps of technology to be realized. The birth of the steel age heralded in the twentieth century and gave us almost unlimited ability to create the comforts and social advantages of machine-produced goods.

Consider the colossal steam hammer invented and built by James Nasmyth, himself a student of James Watt at the Carron Iron Works, where his mentor had fashioned his first engines using cumbersome wooden machinery. Nasmyth's towering hammer and machines could forge glowing one-ton billets of wrought iron and steel into the complicated and complex large parts of engines and machines. Also there was Richard Garrett, whose portable steam engines, traction and road steam engines, steam road rollers and steam cranes would be copied and built throughout the world to till the soils, carve out the roads and thrash the grains.

The first practical sternwheel steamer was built in Scotland by Angus Symington using James Watt's engines as early as 1801, and in 1802 Robert Fulton devised his plan for an American steamer after visiting Symington. In 1806 Boulton and Watt delivered an engine to fit into this vessel which utilized the wheel and machinery devised by Symington, and in 1807 the *Clermont* attained a speed of five knots on the Hudson River. Thus, we have both the first paddlewheel steamer and the first sternwheel steamer successfully powered by James Watt, almost a quarter of a century before *Beaver* arrived out on our coast.

Engines and pumps developed swiftly after the *Beaver*'s creation, and reached a point of perfection in her declining years where simplicity and availability could place them in any man's hands. Many beam and side-lever engines were built after the *Beaver*, but steel cylindrical fire tube boilers quickly replaced her iron box and tube boiler. The vertical engines were often inclined at thirty to forty-five degrees to drive the paddlewheels directly through a connecting rod, rather than indirectly through a walking beam or side lever. But the inverted vertical engine (where

113

the cylinders were mounted above the crankshaft) was developed in many combinations after 1870, as condensing and expansion of steam was more fully utilized with the higher steam pressure produced in steel boilers.

While the *Beaver* had fired the engineer's imagination, it was the railway locomotive that lent design to much of the logging and agricultural steam equipment. But the *Beaver* had come to her demise before many of these reached her area. The tremendous advent of a gold discovery in the province earlier, then the coming of a railroad, had heralded an influx of people from all walks of life, and some of these people brought the knowledge and skills to develop the steam engine into an everyman's tool.

The locomotive boiler was the first self-contained and self-supporting pressure vessel ever built, and it was built extremely strong for the rugged service of its day. Its furnace safely enclosed within the steel water walls of the boiler required no brickwork, and its smoke box and stack lent itself to induced draft created by the exhaust steam or blower that forced a bed of coals to glow hotter than any smithy's forge. It was quickly copied into a form of portable power when fitted with an engine and mounted on large wheels that could be drawn by teams of horses from one location to another over trails no locomotive could ever travel.

When the same boiler-mounted engine drove these wheels, it became a self-moving power plant that could even pull other loaded wagons, thus becoming a traction engine. When fitted with road making or cultivating equipment, it became the most versatile machine ever invented by man to that date, and found many applications where the cost of rails and roadbed would not have justified a railroad. Even the famous caterpillar tractor of today owes its origin to a steam tractor, called a "lumbard", which boasted caterpillar tracks.

George Stephenson's vertical locomotive cylinders were later in the locomotive's development, fitted horizontally onto the frame carrying the boiler. The horsepower machine (a capstan turned by a horse on the end of a long lever to provide mechanical advantage) was one of the first to be improved by this type of engine power.

114

By driving the pinion gear shaft (originally the output shaft) with a small engine, the capstan (the original input shaft, which had been turned by a horse harnessed to its long lever and tugging around in a circle) could now be wrapped with ropes or wires that could lift or pull loads. Later a pair of horizontal engines suitably geared could drive huge horizontal drums or vertical drums onto which the wire working lines were spooled. The whole unit of engines, winding winches and boiler mounted on log skids became known as a donkey engine—a longtime workhorse of western logging, wharf and bridge construction. Another boiler that was self-contained and self-supporting was the Cornish, or Crofton, boiler that was later modified into the Lancashire boiler. Yet they were ignored by the marine engineer and only found great favor in the new industrial facilities where they supplied steam to beam and mill engines, which drove the long line shafts powering the multitude of new machines manufacturing production line goods. This boiler also found great favor in the shallow-draft sternwheel river steamers, as it lent itself to both wood and coal firing and had a very low center of gravity, which their deck-mounted equipment required.

The *Beaver*'s final boiler when her new owners installed it, did not equal either the locomotive or the Cornish boiler. While the pipe boilers of the earlier riverboats were quickly discarded for the above types of boiler, the marine engineer had to await the development of the Scotch marine boiler to realize a really safe self-contained steam maker to take to sea. The *Beaver*'s last boiler was a return tubular design, cylindrical in shape but still requiring a bricked-in furnace to contain its fire and support the boiler above it. It was an off-shot of the local sawmill's demands for an economical steam maker that could be fitted over a large Dutch oven type furnace area, where wet wood waste and chips from the cutting saws could be dried by the heat of the refractory and brought up to ignition temperature all within one combustion chamber.

While the *Beaver*'s new role would contribute another legend, that of the towboat's origin, it was the forthcoming political events that would have the most profound effect on this wilderness frontier. With the departing of the prospectors, and before

115

mining and lumbering began to really contribute to the welfare of British Columbia, the economy settled into a depression that pointed out the need to unite the colonies of Vancouver Island and the mainland. In 1866 this was realized, and control of Vancouver Island by the Hudson's Bay Company was surrendered. In 1867, Russia sold Alaska to the United States of America, and the Americans began a determined fight to evict the Hudson's Bay Company from these prime areas, while redoubling their efforts in the south to secure the San Juan Islands from Britain.

In 1871, after England had released the North West Territories to Canada, John A. Macdonald offered British Columbia complete absolution of their British Treasury debt and the Pacific terminus of a transcontinental railway if they would join his newly created confederation. This met with almost wholehearted support in the west, and the signing of this deed forced the Hudson's Bay Company to release more of its control over the country. This was the political environment as the *Beaver* came into private hands.

CHAPTER FIVE

Marchant's *Beaver* —
An Accident Waiting to Happen

THE *BEAVER*'S FINAL ROLE, AS A TOWBOAT-FREIGHTER, WAS A GRAND finale to a long and exciting career. Her hull and engines were still capable of many years of useful work in this trade, though her boilers suffered constantly from the entrainment of salty water from her jet condenser. When her large deckhouse and rigging were finally chopped down, this problem received first consideration. Little could be done with the jet condenser, but steam could be used more efficiently by replacing the big heavy slide valves on the main engines with a form of poppet valve and refitting the pistons for better sealing—this reduced the volume of steam to be condensed. With much of the housework, the old boiler was lifted out and a new one fitted.

The company entrusted with the refitting job and the man who had created the new boiler were to become synonymous with the high standard of workmanship and the safety record of shipping on this coast. Captain Joseph Spratt's Albion Iron and Ship Repair Works would become even better known in the years ahead as the Victoria Machinery Depot.

But all of this was still in the future in 1874, when certain gentlemen residing in Victoria decided to pool their wealth and buy the *Beaver*. And, what a diversified group of entrepreneurs they were! The Victoria Whaling Adventurer's Club had been formed just a few years earlier to support Captain Thomas Welcome Roys' hunt on this coast for whales with his newly developed whaling gun. Roys had enticed support from a large section of the local business interests, but this new joint ownership of the old *Beaver* attracted an even more unlikely group of investors. Foremost among them were John Stafford, who listed himself as a butcher, and George Rudlin, a highly respected retired mariner. The others were Harry Saunders, a grocer; William Harrison, a porter; Frank Williams, a publican; and, Edwin Coltman, an engineer (engineering had not yet gained the status of a profession and still was considered by the upper classes as a blue collar occupation, we might assume this man to be in civil or mechanical engineering). The last individual to sign the deed was Charles Morton, who felt it sufficient to list himself simply as a "gentleman."

One possible reason for their joint interest in the *Beaver*'s resurrection was CPR's surveyor Marcus Smith's intentions to make a primary survey of Alfred Waddington's former pack trail route for the new railway's right-of-way. The plan was to reach saltwater at the head of Bute Inlet, then island hop via bridges to Vancouver Island at Seymour Narrows, thence southward to Esquimalt. No other piece of legislation was to cause more turmoil or create more speculation than this giant step in joining Canada together.

Near riots and uprisings took place throughout the province, and nowhere was this more visible than in Victoria. Claims of patronage, conniving and outright lying were hurled at the government and their agents. The anger stemmed from the fact that property along the right-of-way for the railway had been bought up by friends of the government, even before the route information became public. The Vancouver Island section designated the Esquimalt and Nanaimo Railway, though approved in principal only, also was discovered to have the property along the right-of-way secured by knowing money. Much of this bad temper was directed at Robert Dunsmuir, the "Coal Tycoon" who eventually built this quaint little railway.

Much anger was also displayed by mainland people who, after agreeing to join the island colony in one large province with one single legislature, found themselves outvoted and the capital moved from New Westminster to Victoria with subsequent drops in mainland property values and business returns. Now it appeared that with the signing of an order-in-council by John A. Macdonald, designating Esquimalt as the terminus, they were to

118

also lose the railway, and both the river city of New Westminster and the infant sawmill town of Granville on Burrard Inlet were to be bypassed and left to fallow in the backwater.

While speculation was rampant on both sides of the Strait of Georgia, and property even around Port Moody had been subdivided and offered to British investors, the greatest cause of this upset was lack of knowledge of the transcontinental railway's intent. None of the known mountain passes provided grades suitable for the railway, and those that might be crossed lay far north of the Fraser River canyon and its difficult route to reach tidewater. Waddington's route (first explored as a possible wagon trail to bring out Cariboo gold in 1863) bypassed the expensive construction of the canyon, but the challenge to skirt the rock-bound sides of Bute Inlet, then jump across some large waterways to reach Vancouver Island, while eagerly agreed to by the population there, caused most knowing people to shake their heads in disbelief.

While the government pondered this difficult decision, the engineer and the gentleman within the *Beaver*'s new group of owners were aware that serious surveys and subdividing were about to commence at the head of Bute Inlet. Such an undertaking required a supply vessel with ample accommodation to house the work crews and carry out map work, at least until a site was cleared ashore. The *Beaver* seemed a logical choice. After hasty preparations, the *Beaver* surreptitiously lifted her anchor out of the mud of James Bay in early November and sailed out into the rain-soaked darkness. A week later, reports filtered back to Victoria of a tent town that had sprung up on the wet foreshore at the head of Bute Inlet, as speculators slashed bracken and fell trees to stake land claims.

Fortunately, saner minds prevailed. Alan Moberly reported that the Fraser River route still was the most practical, the governor general Lord Carnarvon agreed with him after a hurried visit west, so did Alexander Mackenzie in 1878. And finally, after a great deal of waffling back and forth after the Tories swept back into power that fall, so did John A. Macdonald. He offered to build the E & N from Victoria to the coalmines of Cumberland, and commence construction north from Fort Yale through the

119

Fraser Canyon to Shuswap Lake. This appeared to please everyone, especially when a sea link between both railways was assured.

The rush to Bute Inlet died away after this report, and the engineer, the gentlemen and the *Beaver*, returned to Victoria Harbour as quietly as they had left. Within a decade, loggers would crush away the brave pegs and markers of the surveyor's town site in Bute Inlet, cutting massive trees for bridge timbers to carry Onderdonk's section of the CPR up through the tempest canyon.

Born in Essex in 1836, George Rudlin had served his time on the Newcastle coal colliers, before joining the steamer *Victoria* transporting supplies to the British army in the Crimea. After sailing into the Pacific coast trade aboard the brig *London*, he bought the schooner *Circus* and later built the *Discovery* for the lumber trade here, landing lumber from Port Madison mills for the first Presbyterian church built in Victoria. He also carried coal from Nanaimo to Victoria aboard the *Black Diamond*, commanded the iron-hulled steam schooner *Emma* which Captain Roys had used in his whaling gun venture, and the ex-British Navy steam sloop-of-war *Grappler*. He soon proved himself a capable master of the *Beaver*, but first they had to reorganize the company as the British Columbia Towing and Transportation Co. Ltd., with Henry Saunders as chairman. Then the *Beaver* had to shed some of its top hamper and aftercabin, before she could tow in lumber and coal ships from Race Rocks to Granville or Nanaimo, or back to sea again.

To appreciate the reason behind the cutting down of the *Beaver*'s rig, one must take a good look at the sailing ships of those days. Few had the lean sleek lines of the clipper ships, which were then in such favor for fast passenger or valued commodity trade; most were full-bellied, heavily rigged general cargo carriers. Maneuvering a towboat near their overhanging stern or their heavy outboard chain plates, knightheads and bowsprit at their stem, made coming alongside to pass over a towing rope a hazardous occupation-especially in heavy weather or when attempting to warp them into a lumber dock. In a lumber dock, loading was often through a hull opening at bow or stern to accommodate the long lengths of timber that were in such high demand through this period.

The screw-steam tug *Etta White*, built for the Puget Sound lumber trade, was short and lean. Her housework was low and well inboard of her heavy gunwales and rub rails, her funnel short so she could snuggle in close to the large sailing ships she nursed into the mill docks. The *Beaver* was long, wide and high, her masts and her bowsprit in constant conflict with those of the sailing ship she offered to assist. Her one saving grace was her heavy sponson deck that carried the great deck cabin to her full width of forty feet, which protected her vulnerable paddlewheels and allowed her to lay this between the protruding chain plates supporting the sailing ship's tall masts. Both the *Etta White* and the *Beaver* would become role models for future tugboat design, in this area at least.

George Rudlin understood these problems, and with ax and saw he set the crew to work to change forever the quaint little *Beaver* into a distinctive mule of burden. Captain Pender had already removed her heavy yards from the forward mast; now Captain Rudlin sent down her foretopmast and cut off her bowsprit. The mast abaft the funnel was removed in total, and the long, narrow afterdeck cabin was cut back to the boiler fidley area.

Upon this now-open deck, but footed down into the old mast pad, he used part of her former mast to create a heavy set of tow bitts. Satisfied with his much-denuded paddlewheeler, he took her into the towboat trade. When not busy towing, she carried cargos of animals, equipment and supplies around the Straits, or coal scows south from Nanaimo to Victoria and Esquimalt. But the old boilers still plagued her and in late 1876 she went into Spratt's yard to have a full refit.

And what a refit it was! She came out almost a new vessel, hardly recognizable as the old *Beaver*!

The man responsible for this rejuvenation was Captain Joseph Spratt, one of the real old loyalists of the colony and probably one of the best-known early engineers and ship builders on this coast. A few years after this transformation of the *Beaver*, John Irving, son of Captain William Irving, the veteran river pilot who had started the Pioneer Steamboat Line, joined Joe Spratt in the ship repair business. Later Captain John Irving, with Joe as a principal, would form the famous Canadian Pacific Navigation Company, which subsequently was bought out by the CPR early in the new century.

Together, Captains Spratt and Irving built the *Lorne*, the greatest tugboat of her day and in fact, for many years to follow. They incorporated into this tug many of the features found practical from the *Beaver*'s experience. Thus, indirectly at least, as noted earlier, the *Beaver* was the role model for the rather unique design of tugboat that evolved on this coast. Much of this role modeling centered around the *Beaver*'s steering station. While many small schooner hulls lent themselves to being powered with steam for towing purposes, most tried to retain their sternpost steering position with grave mishaps. Even those who moved it forward of the towline bitts, were often in danger, and actually did lose men, when heavy seas came aboard. The raising of the steering station to the top of the main deck cabin and making a windowed cabin forward of the funnel not only protected the helmsman, but also gave him a much clearer view upon which to make judgment commands.

The *Lorne* set a standard of tugboat design that spanned a hundred years, and even today can be seen in our modern fleet of powerful tugs. She boasted steam steering, steam windlasses, triple-expansion engines, two steering stations and a top deck wheelhouse. She enjoyed unheard of creature comforts for her day, such as cabin accommodation for her officers and crew, an officer's saloon complete with a piano, and steam heat throughout. Later she would add other firsts, such as electric lights, steam towing and anchoring winches. Her name honored the new governor general Lord Carnarvon, the Marquis of Lorne, and she was built for Robert Dunsmuir to haul coal scows to Seattle, Vancouver and Victoria, and tow in coal ships from Cape Flattery. Ironically, but quite naturally, this 140-foot colossus and those lesser-sized replicas, which quickly copied her successful design, put the old *Beaver* out of work in the towing trade.

Captain Spratt had entered the coastal navigation picture just as the gold rush waned, but confident business opportunities existed here, he commenced building a 116-foot sidewheel steamer in 1872. Salvaging the engines and boiler from the wrecked steamer *Transport* to install in her, he had just launched the hull in the San Juan Island Territory, when the Emperor of Germany, William 1st, mediating the border claim on behalf of the international court, awarded these islands to the United States of America.

Finding himself an unwilling American resident, Spratt rushed to Esquimalt and demanded Royal Navy protection. HMS Boxer was duly dispatched to the new American territory to tow the recently launched vessel and all her owner's possessions back to Victoria. Locating a site on the west shore of the Upper Harbor near the entrance to the Gorge River, whose picturesque five-mile tidal waterway skirts the northern boundaries of Esquimalt to drain Portage Inlet, Captain Spratt completed the *Maude* then retained his fitter and shipwright to offer ship repair and building services to others.

A modest foundry soon followed this new enterprise on the same site and a company formed, called the Albion Iron Works, whose services were quickly sought and appreciated by the local marine trades. Captain William Grant later built his home and the dock facilities for his Victoria Sealing Company, and later the Canadian Pacific Whaling Company on Bay Street just west of Spratt's yard. Victoria's new electric street railway spanned the Gorge at this point to serve the naval base at Esquimalt. It was this Point Ellice Bridge on Bay Street, overloaded with three streetcars full of holiday families, that collapsed the wooden span with great loss of life on May Day, 1896.

Spratt's 116-foot sidewheeler *Maude* had begun to make a respected name for herself ferrying people from Victoria to Moodyville and Hastings Mill on Burrard Inlet. It also had a good business shuttling settlers to northern ports and the local militia to trouble spots by the time the old *Beaver* arrived at Spratt's dock for refit. With great dispatch he arranged her new look, removing much of her deckhouse, the remnants of her bowsprit and masts. With the deck open to the elements, the old boilers were broken up and lifted out of her and a new, large single-steel boiler, built right in his engineering works, was installed.

This was a revolutionary new approach in boiler construction and its design probably was a forerunner of the famous Scotch marine type, which would be the accepted standard for marine boilers for the next 100 years. Spratt's unique boiler was a horizontal, cylindrical return tubular type with a large, separate steam drum fitted off the top and a smaller mud drum off the bottom. The whole weight of this unit was suspended within a large brick furnace having two sets of fire doors. The large common fire grates directed the flames upward against the bottom of the main drum, while the products of combustion reached her funnel by passing through steel tubes fitted between the boiler heads, which were themselves surrounded by the water within the boiler shell. The steam collection drum was cast slightly upward to ensure the driest steam reached her engines; to augment this, the steam from the upper drum was lead through a strong steel collar that acted as a drier and also carried the weight of the funnel upon it.

The boiler faced the engines and the return tubes led the products of combustion forward to her uptake and smoke box, which placed her new funnel more forward than her original. This allowed the new large tow bitts to be fitted much closer to her turning point and her paddlewheels. This gave her great maneuverability. The crowning achievement that really made her a great tugboat was a unique clutch that Spratt designed and fitted to her paddlewheel shaft. The clutch allowed one engine to work independent of the other or in unison; with one paddlewheel turning in reverse and the other ahead, the rejuvenated *Beaver* could spin literally right around in her own length.

While few other boats in the world could match this achievement, this clutch feature could well have been responsible for her final loss and, sufficient to note here, was not fitted to other side-wheelers. Of course, it was the new boiler that really made all this possible. With steam pressure almost six times greater than her original boiler's output, her ancient engines refitted with disc-type poppet valves, creating far less friction then her former large heavy slide valves, she could thrash her paddlewheels up to an impressive ten knots in loaded trim or tow a loaded sailing ship to sea at an equally impressive six knots.

The *Beaver* now began creating her last and most-remembered legend as the hard-working handmaiden serving the growing coastal settlements and the ever-increasing number of sailing ships arriving to take away their lumber and coal.

Her new master was the great-grandfather of Art Warren, a very competent master mariner this writer had as his mentor when serving his time as a budding seaman in this same trade. Captain James D. Warren hailed from Prince Edward Island and was a daring, dedicated mariner with more than a decade of service on the West Coast before investing in the *Beaver* and becoming her master. His chief engineer was Benjamin Madigan, who had supervised all the new repairs and innovations, and the second engineer was John Fullerton.

After a shakedown cruise, which was reported with a certain awe by the local media of the day, they took in tow the large bark *Wellington*, laden with a full cargo of coal for San Francisco. Three days later the *Beaver* crept back into Victoria, looking a little less jaunty than she had when the reporters saw her last. Her tall funnel was gone and her port paddlewheel was badly damaged. The sailing ship *Henry Buck*, while being towed north to Nanaimo through Dodd's Narrows, had rammed her. Captain Warren's gamble with the current in this notorious tidal bore hadn't paid off, and that would cost him a few days' lost earnings in the shipyard.

Even in those early days of towing, competition was becoming keen for this work, and a master had to use every advantage he could muster to complete his tow quickly and solicit another without lost time. There were many strange crafts offering their services as towboats, most were improvised from hulls built for a sailing rig. Some, like the old *Union*, were built on scowlike vessels, and all offered to tow or carry freight at less than the other guy. All were chancy transportation at best, but their cost could always be haggled upon unless dire necessity or a lack of competition gave the "tower" a decided advantage over the "towee."

When the *Beaver* had been built, her hull had been designed around the standard bluff sailing vessel lines of that day; but as steam engines and stern propellers evolved, at least on this coast,

125

they were often fitted into vessels of much finer lines, such as the small sleek schooners that were readily available. These were of an Appledore design that had gained great popularity on the East Coast where they were built in large numbers for the fishery, and also as packet vessels in the Atlantic trade. Some arrived out here to follow the local whale and sealing fisheries during latter part of the nineteenth century, but many more were built here by the shipwrights and sailors who had gambled on making a fortune during the gold rush. When a heavy boiler, engine and water and fuel spaces had been fitted into these fine-lined hulls, there was little room for crew or comfort and damn little for freeboard to keep the sea out.

Steering was aft of the small fidley house, which covered over the boiler and engine, and the tow bitts were wedged in behind that. This was not a very handy position for control of a steam tug and tow. Historically, it was the position from which command was directed in a sailing vessel because it was close to the rudderstock where a tiller or a rope-drive steering wheel could be fitted and a watch kept on the sails and wind. Unfortunately, it was also the spot most exposed to weather and waves; the area was hazarded by a towline that could flip a man over the side of the boat or break his bones at any time. With a funnel and deckhouse blocking the view forward, it also hindered the safe piloting of the ship. Many of these earlier towboaters experienced maiming, loss of life or overwhelming of the ship from this cause. The *Beaver*'s arrangement proved better in all ways and few tugs or small steamers retained their aft-deck steering after this time, except for emergency conditions.

The *Beaver*'s next accident, though of minor consequence, almost resulted in a fatal collision with the large sailing vessel she was taking to sea. Elizabeth Winsby, daughter of Henry Saunders who was then president of the BC Towing and Transportation Company, recalled the incident for the *Victoria Colonist*. Benjamin Madigan was chief engineer and Captain J. D. Warren was master. "They were nearing Cape Flattery when the barometer began to fall in an ominous manner, and soon after a gale sprung up. The master of the sailing ship became very anxious to have his ship free of the restrictive towline, so he could

126

set sail and get his ship out into the safety of the broad ocean. But communications were difficult under those conditions and it finally took a signal gun and flag hoist to get the *Beaver*'s attention."

The heavy floatable rope towlines of those days before the advent of steam capstans or winches were usually laid out fore and aft on the decks of the towing vessel. The eye on the end of this was passed to the vessel to be towed and lashed to her anchor windlass or forward mooring bitts, so it could be quickly released at the sailing vessel's discretion. The standard procedure adopted at that time was to signal the tug of their intention to drop the towline, after they had set sufficient sails to ensure headway on the ship. The tug would then sheer off to one side of the overtaking ship, usually the windward side. The ship would then slip the towline and sail on, leaving the tug to slow down as her crew hauled in the tow line, walking it the full length of her decks and flaking it down ready for the next tow.

The short notice given of this intention, and the swift passage of the sailing ship under the violent blast of this wintry southeaster, caused the two ships to close at an alarming rate. *Beaver*, frantically aware she had a runaway charging down on her, hauled around beam-on to the large seas kicked up by the weather tide conditions and scooted madly to get clear. Unfortunately, at the very same time the sailing ship's spanker wore across the wind with an unholy crash causing the larger vessel, still not fully under way, to sheer toward the wildly threshing *Beaver*.

Elizabeth Winsby continues her account of this strange mishap. "For a few seconds the *Beaver* found herself under the bows of the plunging ship, before she managed to scramble clear. During this awful brief moment, the sailing ship's bows plunged downwards as a steep sea lifted her stern, and in a thrice the end of her long bowsprit caught the *Beaver*'s whistle on the front of the funnel, then rearing up snatching it away from the pipe it had been fitted to.

"The much smaller *Beaver* quickly scooted from under this wildly gyrating extension of the sailing ship, and the ship raced off to sea with the *Beaver*'s whistle firmly grasped by the dolphin striker stay. But the *Beaver* began to lose steam through the opened pipe and Mister Madigan had to whittle a wooden plug and drive this into the pipe with a heavy hammer to conserve steam, so the *Beaver* could battle the gale and get back to port. Years later the *Beaver*'s whistle was returned by the sailing ship's captain, I recall my father kept it for a long time, then I believe it was given to the Victoria museum."

Her account also mentioned the salt encrusted in the *Beaver*'s boiler and how it had to be rigorously blown out from time to time. The *Beaver* still relied on her jet condenser to reduce backpressure of her exhaust steam, and this quenching water was drawn from the sea. Thus, the feeding of this condensate back into the boiler, where its evaporation concentrated these solids, saw her boiler water got saltier and saltier until the engineer blew down a few inches from the boiler and replaced that amount with fresh water from the tanks.

Though the *Beaver* pioneered the ship-towing business, as more ships arrived for the coal and lumber trade within the Straits of Georgia and Puget Sound, more towing type boats were built. Many were built by the companies in these trades, but most were independent and offered their services to the highest bidder. As more towboats vied for this business in later years, it was often the sailing shipmaster that could select his tug from the lowest bidder. In those days of little or no communication, the master was officially the ship's agent and entered into contracts concerning his ship, cargo or crew, which were quite binding in any court of law.

Before the advent of large powerful towing vessels had arrived, the *Beaver* under Captain J. Warren, and those others like the *Maude* and *Otter*, kept themselves gainfully employed in the freight and passenger business or towing such mundane things as log rafts or small scows loaded with livestock or equipment. Ocean-going vessels requiring a tow into port usually arrived off the Race or anchored in Pedder Bay or off Royal Roads and waited while a steamship could be arranged to accommodate them. This suited the *Beaver* well, but it was a position neither ship owners or mill owners were satisfied with. Thus, it wasn't long until the larger lumber and coal producers built tugs to service their business and arranged with the shipping companies to

128

ensure only their tugs or those authorized by them brought the sailing ships into their facilities. This, plus the reluctance of many master mariners to bring their larger ships into the temperamental, tide and gale swept Straits of Juan de Fuca, caused enterprising tug masters to go out farther to Cape Beale or even to Cape Flattery to solicit towing business.

And it was this soliciting by steam tugs through these later years of the sailing vessel that created many interesting incidents and the rate wars mentioned earlier. These events would resolve themselves into one or the other of the following scenarios. First, the shipmaster might find himself off this virtual graveyard of the Pacific, in lightly ballasted trim with contrary winds and an onshore set of currents. His position was very vulnerable. If a tugboat—anybody's tugboat—was within hailing distance, prudence would force the master to take a towline regardless of how steeply the tugboat master set the price. Shipmasters who tried to barter a better rate, found the rate escalating the closer his ship set toward the offshore dangers. Few mariners after thousands of miles of sea travel would hazard their ship just to save a few dollars. This was the ideal condition for a tug master who could make himself a few extra dollars from another mariner's vulnerability.

The other scenario was when the sailing shipmaster felt he had the advantage, and used this to get a bargain-towing rate. When more than one tug was in sight of his landfall, or favorable winds and currents allowed him to continue his voyage into the Straits and possibly all the way to safe anchorage off Port Angeles or Victoria, he would condescend to a disinterested haggle with the tug master who would sail up alongside. Sometimes he could entice the tug master to accompany him toward this safety, knowing full well the more miles he cut out of the towing distance the less he'd be charged, yet if his gamble backfired and conditions became adverse, he had the tug nearby to pull his chestnuts from the fire. A canny shipmaster could reduce the normal rates by more than 50 percent by using his advantage to disdainfully reject any small consideration offered by the tug master. But he kept a weather eye on the tugboat and the sea conditions. If another sailing ship hoved up over the horizon, or if tide and wind appeared to becoming adverse, he'd quickly settle on the best offer, and the tug would pass over the towline and move up forward to take her in tow.

Sometimes it was the tug master who growled in anguish when he cleared the bulk of the sailing ship, to find that a much larger ship with possibly a more anxious master was flying the signals requesting a tug as she hoved to a few miles off. Sometimes it was the shipmaster, who found a tug or two steaming toward him after he'd taken a towline at an outrageous towing charge or played the conditions too long and lost both the weathercock and the tugboat, and had to pay dearly to be extricated. But one condition always was honored in this business, once a bargain was verbally struck between tugboat master and sailing shipmaster, it was carried out to the letter.

Much of this took place after the *Beaver* proved the way that a tow boat should be laid out with a clear deck aft for handling the towline and with that towline fastened to a towing post well forward of the rudder, so the vessel's stern could be turned under it and not restricted by it, and with engine controls and steering forward of the funnel, above all deck obstruction, and well clear of boarding seas. The *Lorne* and later such longtime favorites as the *Haro, Queen, Active* and *Sea Lion* would further set the style and standard that are still accepted as necessary today.

The industry really became competitive after the Americans built huge powerful tugs to support their expanding lumber trade. Each large lumber company had tugs waiting off Cape Flattery to bring in ships to their Puget Sound mill towns. These tugmasters were not averse to soliciting any other towing business during their moments of idleness, and this forced Canadian tugs to offer better services just to survive.

At first, the *Beaver* found ample customers waiting off the Race or Royal Roads near Victoria in those earlier years, and towed them at her convenience to Nanaimo, New Westminster or Granville (Vancouver, as it became known in 1886), for a rewarding $350 return. When business really got mean as the years went by, she had to drop her price to $150 just to maintain her upkeep and payroll.

August of 1877 witnessed the passing away of the "Father of British Columbia." Sir James Douglas, who had dedicated his life in the service of the HBC and the province of British Columbia, by holding the highest office of each, was dead. He was struck down by a simple flu virus while far away from medical help in the still rather wild interior of the province he had guided into self-reliance. Many of his early initiatives still survive today, such as the public school system, which he introduced in the form of a HBC school, and the missionary schools that he supported through the Hudson's Bay Company, which brought education to the ordinary peoples in the wilds. The legislative assembly was another of his plans, which he originally sponsored and had to cajole responsible citizens to join so they could finally realize self-government. The diversification of HBC interest into coal, transportation and industry, and their final disposition into private hands, were things he could justly take credit for.

Through the efforts of Simpson and Douglas the Hudson's Bay Company grew into maturity and set the standards and credibility that would be their hallmark of fame, and one which later companies, such as the CPR, would follow to create their own hallowed image. The *Beaver* had lost two staunch supporters in the passing away of Douglas and Simpson, for both had supported the new age of steam and, on the West Coast at least, had proven its commercial viability. Now the *Beaver* would carry on alone for a few more years.

Captain Tom Pamphlet was born at Barking, in Essex, England, and commanded the *Beaver* in 1876 when she carried as cargo a large black bear that had become a problem around Gastown. It was to be delivered to Owen's market in Victoria to be made into bear burgers, but the bear didn't appreciate the pun and broke loose aboard ship and terrorized the crew. Capt. Pamphlet managed to secure it with handcuffs after it had jammed its head through a tiny window into the crew's eating area.

Captain Pamphlet had been master of the schooner *Meg Merrilees* in 1860, when he carried Captain Edward Stamp (Stamp Mills) and Gilbert Sproat (Sproat Lake) to Port Alberni where they established a water-powered sawmill. In 1864 aboard

131

the steam tug *Diana* (actually a former small steam launch from China, which had been built for the Pacific Mail Company), Captains Pamphlet and Stamp inspected a site in Burrard Inlet (north end of Dunlevy St.) for a new steam-powered sawmill.

The first shipment of machinery for the mill was lost at sea, so they had to wait a full year for more to be built and sent out around the Horn. Thus, it wasn't until 1867 that Stamp's mills began cutting 30,000 board feet of timber and lumber a day. During the interim, 150-foot Douglas firs were fell by Jeremiah Rogers at Jerry's Cove on Point Grey (now Jericho Beach) and towed to the harbor mill site, where they were hewed by ax into spars and heavy deals of timber, and loaded through bow or stern doors into large sailing ships.

Thomas Pamphlet meanwhile had become master of the first steam tugboat to be built in the territory. Captain Stamp spent $50,000 to have the 100-foot sidewheel steamer *Isabel*, built in 1866 at Victoria, to tow sailing ships in and out of Burrard Inlet. Sewell Prescott Moody (Moodyville), who had dismantled his water-powered mill at Sooke and rebuilt it on the north shore of the inlet, actually began cutting lumber a year before Stamp got his steam-powered mill running. Ten years later, his Pioneer Sawmills at Moodyville bought the former Puget Sound built propeller-driven steam tug *Etta White* for the same job, as well as log yarding and log towing.

The year following his command of the fine new steamer *Isabel*, Captain Pamphlet presented himself to Captain Pender to be examined as pilot. Along with Captains Gardener and Titcomb, he was appointed to pilot deep-water vessels into the ports of Esquimalt, Victoria, Nanaimo and Burrard Inlet. However, the Pilot Board revoked this license in 1874, because the good captain had been absent from duty without leave.

In these early days before the advent of postal service, wireless or telephone, communication was a very chancy and often delayed affair. As noted earlier, vessels could wait for days for a tug to appear while lying off a lee shore, but tugs could wait even longer for a ship to finally arrive, even though the vessel might have sent ahead notice of her departure and expected date of landfall. Pilots also suffered the same dilemma, and often spent

132

many days rolling around in a tiny pilot boat waiting on station for their charge to appear. Later, pilot stations were created ashore at certain points to which the vessel requiring a pilot would stand-off flying a pilot flag. Banfield Cove, inshore of Cape Beale was one of these off the West Coast, another was located outside Burrard Inlet for local pilots familiar with the tidal currents and shoals of the Narrows to await a ship. This latter spot was located in what was locally known as Skunk Cove because weather disturbances around Point Atkinson, usually surged into it making it a skunky or nasty place to lie at anchor. Dignified on later charts as Pilot's Cove, it is today better known as Caulfield's Cove, for the restful quaint village that grew up around it (sometimes written Caulfeild).

At the time Pamphlet's license was revoked, the pilot duty station was still at William's Head, inside the Race, and the good captain had left the station while on duty for an emergency trip into Victoria—just before a ship stood in and signaled for a pilot. Considering the circumstances, and that the ship had only been delayed not endangered, Judge Gray rescinded the revocation. The following year the *Colonist* noted that Captain Pamphlet pilot's license had been annulled. The cause was the grounding of the steamship *City of Panama*, where else, but on Beaver Rock (Discovery Passage, entrance to Seymour Narrows).

While the *Beaver* did strike some rocks in Howe Sound and was beached at Deep Cove (now Snug Cove) on Bowen Island, before being towed to Victoria for repairs, and in 1880 a shipboard fire burnt away much of her upper housework, it wasn't until 1883 under command of Captain John F. Jagers that she survived her first sinking. Inbound from Victoria with cargo for Hastings Mill, and feeling her way through a dense fog for the Narrows, she struck the rocks laying north of Ferguson Point and went down by the head, her stern still trapped on a sharp rock.

John Jagers was born in East Prussia, his grandfather fought for Napoleon; his uncle took him to sea carrying Baltic timber to London. As second mate of the ship *Gondolier* he arrived at Victoria in 1878. He served for two years as mate of the *Beaver* before taking over command from Captain J. D. Warren, following repairs after the aforesaid fire. Possibly his greatest towing feat with the *Beaver* was a boom of logs that measured more than 100 feet wide and 800 feet long, approximately fifty sections of four-foot diameter logs, picked up in Chemainus on a Thursday evening and delivered to Victoria on Saturday evening.

Using camel floats, the tug *Pilot* raised the old *Beaver* and beached her near where the Bayshore Hotel now is located in Vancouver's harbor. Camel floats, were tanks that could be flooded and sunk either side of the stricken vessel then attached together with cable or chain under the sunken ship. Pumped out, they offered buoyancy so a vessel could be towed into the shallow water near the beach at high water; at low water, hopefully, the ship could be patched up so she would float, then be towed to a shipyard for more permanent repairs.

With her hull watertight, *Beaver* was towed to Victoria and sold by BC Towing and Transportation to offset her $7,500 repair bill. Robert Paterson Rithet, a former San Francisco businessman quickly becoming one of the capital city's merchant princes of the day, acquired the *Beaver* in relatively sound condition by default for pennies on the pound, and offered it to his friend Henry Saunders. Henry, agreeing to manage the ship, sold controlling interest in the *Beaver* to Edgar Crow-Baker, then offered George Marchant command of the vessel. Almost four years had passed since the sinking, and many important events had passed on into history, before Captain Marchant brought the *Beaver* back to Vancouver.

During the mid-1880s, the building of the CPR east through the mountains from Port Moody by Andrew Onderdonk and the construction of the E & N Railway by Robert Dunsmuir on Vancouver Island created a great demand for timber, lumber and ties. Loggers searched farther and farther up the coast to find suitable logs to supply the mills that cut the massive bridge timbers, rail ties, tunnel cribbing, station and service building lumber. Carrying supplies up to these loggers, and towing their log booms south to the mills, had kept the *Beaver* and many other steam tugs gainfully employed.

But as completion of the railway project loomed ever closer, much of this employment began to disappear. Henry Saunders felt the *Beaver* might be employed carrying railway passengers

134

and their freight to up coast ports. He applied for, and got, a passenger license for the *Beaver*. What was remarkable about this was the fact that fifteen years earlier the Hudson's Bay Company hadn't felt her worthy of being upgraded for this service.

In a letter to London in 1873, Chief Factor Grahame stated in part, "the *Beaver* is old and her upper works considerably weather beaten–since the imposition of the requirements of the Canadian Steamship Laws, the alterations necessary to qualify her for a certificate for a passenger boat would cause considerable expense, I suggest she be offered for sale."

Henry Saunders hedged his bet on this passenger business, by offering Hastings Mill a contract to service their logging camps and tow their logs south to the mill. Captain George Marchant was his ace in the hole, for George had been a longtime master of their tugs and knew their camp locations well.

George Marchant was born in Cornwall in 1844, and joined the Royal Navy in 1858. He arrived at Esquimalt aboard HMS *Zealous* in 1867. Becoming a member of the *Beaver*'s navy crew he sailed north with Lt. Pender to chart Portland Canal. His discovery of a dangerous rock in Hecate Straits caused Captain Pender to have it surveyed into the chart and named after the finder. After the *Beaver* was decommissioned in December, 1870, George Marchant took command of an unusual vessel—a locally built paddlewheel steamer by the name *Union*.

Scow-shaped and powered by the boiler and engine from a threshing machine, which ran in only one direction, the *Union* could barely make five knots. It earned the unflattering nickname of "Sudden Jerk." For a time the ship ran a ferry service across Burrard Inlet, between Moodyville and Gastown. In 1876 George Marchant left the *Union* to join Captain Warren as mate of the *Beaver*, a job he carried out till 1878 when he joined Hastings Mill towing logs with the steam tug *Pilot*.

Through most of these years, much talk was made about the new railway and the business it would bring to the port. Finally in May of 1880, work commenced on the Yale Tunnel into the Fraser Canyon, and a right-of-way between Emory Bar and Fort Yale that would stretch more than a hundred miles northward to Savona. About 5,000 tons of steel rail had been moved into

Emory Creek, at the head of navigation the previous year by the sternwheelers *Royal City, Reliance* and *Glenora*. On May 3, 1881, the first steam locomotive arrived at New Westminster. Christened the *Yale No 1*, the thirty-ton engine was carefully rolled onto the foredeck of the tired old *Royal City* for the run up to Emory Bar, her crew ringing the locomotive's bell as they passed each whistle stop.

Most everyone hoped the new railway would arrive out on the coast at Burrard Inlet, but until the provincial government allotted a right-of-way consistent with that offered throughout the other provinces, the CPR refused to even look beyond the bustling railway construction town of Port Moody to fulfill their mandate. The Royal Navy, after having the Central Park timber stand allocated to their use for masts, spars and yards had dedicated Port Moody as a mainland base for protection of the colony. Its ice-free harbor was connected up with New Westminster through a wagon trail (North Road) built by a royal engineer. Thus, William Van Horne could declare this small, sheltered saltwater harbor as the western terminus of the CPR, though fully aware any connecting marine link would have to traverse two sets of difficult tidal narrows. He continued to use it as a ploy till the people of Granville pleaded for a court of last appeal.

This was in fact out-and-out political blackmail. Though it satisfied the railway's federal contract to span this great land from sea to sea with ribbons of steel rail, and undoubtedly made many people who had bought up real estate in Port Moody extremely happy, it was not what the rest of the lower mainland wanted or expected as their perk for joining in confederation and giving eastern businesses access to Pacific trade. The residents of Granville petitioned Premier William Smithe, offering to incorporate their community, pay provincial taxes on a properly surveyed and laid out town site if he would offer the proper enticement to Van Horne to extend the railway at least another twelve miles west into the beautiful harbor of Burrard Inlet. To sweeten the offer, "The Three Greenhorns," as Morton, Hailstone and Brighouse had been nicknamed, agreed to give up a large chunk of their preempted 550 acres west of Granville Street to the CPR. The government, still smarting from the loss of the terminus at

Victoria, finally agreed to dicker on their behalf with Van Horne.

In February 1886, William Cornelius Van Horne was invited to come and personally view the property offered in lieu of the usual twenty-mile right-of-way, and was reported as exclaiming "What a wonderful location for a seaport!" Suggesting it should have a name commensurate with its dignity and importance, he offered the name of Vancouver to commemorate the first white man to visit it. He accepted all they had generously offered, signed an agreement of intent to continue his railway westward, then showed them a drawing his engineers had prepared months before Port Moody had even been publicly designated as the terminus. On this the proposed marine terminus was not in Burrard Inlet as he had intimated, but in English Bay where deepwater ships such as he envisioned plying the Orient trade could land without fighting the tides of either First or Second Narrows. With this thrilling description, the people of Granville generously gave him a right-of-way for his railway through the center of their town!

Altogether, Van Horne's visit netted the CPR the property west of Granville offered by the Green Horns and several hundreds of acres throughout the lower mainland offered by the provincial government, including all that area west of what is now Boundary Road and south of 49th Avenue. From the citizens of Granville he was gifted an area north of False Creek for freight yards and equipment servicing plus a right-of-way along Burrard Inlet, and thence right through the center of their township over a rail trestle spanning False Creek to Greer's Beach, which is known today as Kitsilano, where he had proposed to build his deepwater dock.

Certain city fathers such as Robson, Powell and the Oppenheimer brothers were pleased to accede to these demands, and carried the vote. In April of that year, the city of Vancouver was duly incorporated. In May, Mayor M. A. Maclean and his ten elected aldermen were sworn into office.

New Westminster, still smarting from its loss of capital city status, was incensed even more by being so blatantly ignored in this deal, and their anger was only slightly reduced by Van Horne's magnanimous offer to build a branch line southward into

137

their river city. J. J. Hill, building his Great Northern Railway west from Chicago, rubbed his hand with glee at New Westminster's predicament; he was convinced he could gain them as an ally when he was ready to pull strings in B.C.'s provincial government. With his all-American route passing through Steven's Pass to arrive at salt water near the mill town of Everett, and his road crews driving both a spur line southward to Tacoma to connect up with the Southern Pacific, and another north to Blaine and the international border, he knew he could offer New Westminster and the south Fraser Valley a greater service than the CPR. The CPR had selected to build their railroad down the less-developed northern shore of the Fraser.

Hill leased several small Canadian logging railroads that wound through the timbered hills of Surrey south of the Fraser River and spliced them together to reach Port Mann. Then leasing some old service cars and a small *0-4-0* haystacked logging locomotive to run on this narrow gauge line, he provided a railcar barge for his expected freight customers and a luxuriant sternwheeler service for his hoped-for passengers from this irate shipping port.

Jim Hill's glee evolved from a long-standing rivalry with William Van Horne. The animosity had surfaced after their plan to milk the budding CPR, by forcing it south of the Great Lakes and onto Hill's road, had been sabotaged by Van Horne siding with George Stevens and Donald Smith to build an all-Canadian route through the Great Cambrian Shield. Then to add salt to the injury, Van Horne deliberately, and against the advice of the railway's master planner Ian Flemming, ran his westward prairie line close to the border to deny Hill revenue from this source.

In retaliation, Jim Hill rushed his railroad across the northern United States, hoping to secure the Orient silk and passenger trade before the CPR could reach tidewater. The Canadian railroad, spanning half a continent without a principal city or major shipper, was very dependent on servicing this potential market to stay solvent.

But out on the West Coast during the summer of 1886, while land clearing was being carried out on the CPR's newly acquired rail yard property south of Pender Street, a sudden morning wind

138

fanned the sluggishly burning slash fires, carrying sparks and flaming debris into the nearby dry bush and shacks. It was June 13, a calm, hot early Sunday morning with few people up and about, no attendant at the fire sites, and no water available to dose the small fires the sparks created, when this near gale force wind sprung up.

By Sunday afternoon, the city of Vancouver was doomed. Few people attempted to fight the fire, and those that did or those that paused to save prized possessions, found themselves cut off from escape and had to take refuge in the stream that ran through where Columbia Street is today. With neither equipment nor water at hand, the flames leaped through the streets of wooden buildings, driving before them the frightened populace with just the clothes on their backs.

Many fled toward Burrard Inlet. Some were fortunate enough to be ferried out by small boats to the anchored lumber bark *Dunsmuir* or other anchored vessels waiting to berth at Stamp's Mill. Others fled eastward to where the waters of False Creek made a shallow bay near where the Ivanhoe Hotel now sits on Main Street. Covered in water to their necks, people waited out the long hours of night until the fires died down and they could shiver back to solid ground. Unfortunately, Captain Marchant had taken the *Beaver* up to Quadra Island, and didn't return for several days.

On Monday, June 14, Vancouver began to rise from the smoldering ashes; tents were put up and the people returned to rebuild. By Wednesday the first buildings had sprung up on Cordova Street. Vancouver was back in business, even if much was conducted in tents. Just twenty days later on July 4, 1886, and just one minute off her time, the first official train rolled into Port Moody, and less than a year later Vancouver finally came of age as a great seaport.

On May 23, 1887, the *Countess of Dufferin*, locomotive #374 of the Canadian Pacific Railway, garlanded with flowers, puffed up to the newly built deep-sea wharf at the foot of Granville Street with the first transcontinental passenger train behind her, thus proving dominion of a great nation, which stretched out over 4,000 miles to touch both seas. More than 2,000 spectators were on hand for the celebration, and the newly formed fire brigade paraded behind Vancouver's first civic band. On June 14, the *Abysinnia*, first CPR steamer from the Orient landed at this dock with 102 passengers, three bags of mail and 2,800 tons of freight, mostly tea. The *Beaver* saw little of this, as she spent much of her time away from Vancouver, then the following year she, too, was gone.

While Captain George Marchant had been licensed as a knowledgeable coasting pilot, he, like Captain Pamphlet, had trouble retaining this coveted position. His troubles occurred not for lack of talent, he had proven his skills many times over, but for lack of attention to the safe passage of the vessel he had been entrusted with. This was to be the enigma of this otherwise great mariner—his periodic moments of inattention. He had lost his job with Hastings Mills because he grounded their new large tug *Belle* off Sandheads, where she laid over and filled. This, in an area he knew like the back of his hand, having towed many log booms around to the river or up to Burrard Inlet for Gilley Brothers logging the Nicomekl River in the Boundary Bay area.

The last moments of the *Beaver* in his hands proved no exception to his fatal lack of attention affliction, but what makes it all so mysterious is that he never seemed to lack for a command. A few years later, on Dominion Day 1900, he sank the brand new tug *Superior* by causing her to founder in the flooding tiderip off Brockton Point, right in Vancouver's harbor! Lloyd Gore was engineer that trip (of Young and Gore Towing Co.) he survived by diving out the engineroom window and scrambling onto the rocks of Burnaby Shoal. Marchant claimed he was taking a short cut over to Hasting Mill. A local editorial of that time laconically remarked that George Marchant had created a record of sorts–he had managed to sink the oldest and one of the newest steamships on this coast!

It was under the command of this man that the *Beaver* returned to Vancouver carrying settlers and supplies north to Quadra Island and beyond and towing scows or logs south to the city. He did this without any noticeable problem for over a year. Then the *Beaver* paddled out through First Narrows for the last

140

time during the night of July 26, 1888, forging against the last two hours of what had been an extremely large flood tide.

Beaver's hold and deck were laden with freight; she was outward bound to Nanaimo for bunkers of coal before heading north. Some claimed a summer's fog was present as she paddled through the darkness of the Narrows. Other wags claimed afterwards that the fog must only have been in *Beaver*'s wheelhouse. Whatever the conditions, Marchant's report states that a decision to return to Vancouver for some missing cargo was made before the *Beaver* had fully cleared the Narrows, and when she was put about, took the ground on the rocks below Observatory Point.

One should look at this accident from the point of view of a mariner and engineer and examine the hazards as they existed at that time by referring to a pilot's guide of that era. Some daylight navigational aids had been erected and some minor dredging had been carried out to assist both the CPR's chartered Orient vessels and those of Captain Irving's Canadian Pacific Navigation ships. No echo boards or lights had yet been erected when the *Beaver* made her last voyage. Ironically, a watched light was quickly built and put into service within half a cable of this rather sad loss. It was so placed behind the rock cliff that an inbound vessel had to stand well north of this offshore hazard to open or see the light (remember our bearings-in-transit explanation) before proceeding into the Narrows, and it was easily visible to any vessel clearing Brockton Point outbound. Officially, no investigation was carried out on what first appeared as a minor grounding, as it was expected the *Beaver* would remain there for no more than a change of tide. Thus, much of what we know now is gleaned from newspaper accounts of the day, from old mariner's tales or from outright barroom gossip, some of it very suspect.

One thing is quite certain, the *Beaver* was an old boat by this time barely worthy of salvage; newer and better ships had taken away much of her former trade and her present owners had been eking out the last dollars this tired old lady could earn. This is certainly borne out by this writer's inspection of her boiler, some ninety years later. The Spratt-built boiler had been raised from the wreck at the turn of the century and displayed at the original site of Fort Nisqually west of Tacoma, with the steam drum and mud drum still attached.

When I viewed it, in its new location at Point Defiance Park in Tacoma, only the main boiler shell and heavy tube sheets had survived the years of exposure to the weather. The tubes, steam and mud drums had all rusted away and been discarded before the move. But what was of keen interest to me were the number of well-rusted tube stoppers I found still in place through her tube sheets, though most of the tubes themselves had eroded and fallen down into the bottom of the shell. A good engineer would certainly attempt to bring a vessel back into port with a tube stopper sealing a leaking boiler fire tube, but he would never consider taking one to sea in that condition when any capable boilermaker could cut out the leaking tube with a cold chisel, and roll in a new tube, all in an afternoon's work. The fact that I found not one but nine of these tube stoppers still in place proves the *Beaver*, in her final days, had neither talented engineers nor sufficient funds to make seaworthy repairs. And she must have sailed more than once out to sea with some of these tube stoppers in place. She was in fact an accident waiting to happen. Her crew, undoubtedly, were composed from those waterfront ranks unable to find anything better, even though many jobs on the large fleet of newer and more efficient vessels were advertised.

An account given years later by her second engineer, W. H. Evans, was a little vague on vital detail due in some respect I suspect to his age at the time of writing, but more possibly deliberate to avoid placing any blame on him or others who sailed with him on the *Beaver*. The pertinent points of his recall were thus: "It was dark, and from the time we left, till we was on the rocks, was very short." Then he added, "I think I was having a little sleep at the time and don't actually know who was aboard." About the accident, "I think the tide was pretty near high water, but still running in, because the Captain was hugging the south shore pretty tight to get by the eddy off Observation Point [Prospect Point]. The first thing I knew, she hit hard and that settled it, we all got off. We waded ashore and walked through the bush back to the Sunnyside Hotel, from where we had just said our good-byes a few hours before."

142

Historically, second engineers and mates stand the least enjoyable hours in the marine watch system, the early morning and afternoon hours, usually from midnight to daylight, and noon till supper. The master and chief engineer usually enjoy the more reasonable watch hours after breakfast and after supper. They, of course, being seniors, are always on call when trouble or difficulties arise. Thus, while the master might still be on the bridge until his vessel was clear of the hazardous channel, the second engineer should presumably not have been asleep but standing by his engines in case of maneuvers.

The other odd thing about Mr. Evan's account of the accident was his lack of recall about any engine movements or any effort to secure the ship after her grounding or to stand by her, though all pictures surviving show her starboard anchor chain hanging down into the rocks. We know the *Beaver* was fitted with a form of clutch on her paddle shaft, which would allow each engine to turn a paddlewheel independent of the other. We know she had turned fully around within her own length many times before this accident using the engines independently (i.e., one ahead, the other reversing). We know that, even in those days, the navigable channel of First Narrows off Prospect Point was at least one cable wide (600 ft.). We also know the total distance the *Beaver* covered that night, from her dock to her grounding spot, was less than three miles and not all of this was against the flood tide. Presumably, Mr. Evans had retired to his berth well before the ship sailed, to be so heavily drugged with sleep as to not hear any engine maneuvers just a few feet away from his ear nor feel any compunction to enter the engine room and take up his duties.

Both north and south shores of First Narrows during that time shoaled in places for at least one cable out into the channel. This was very pronounced off the Capilano River on the northern shore, where a rocky bench extended eastward to Calamity Spit before spreading out farther to the east in a large, drying mud flat. It was still that way when I grew up there, and we kept a Columbia River fishing boat in one of the many marshy sloughs at that spot.

On the south shore westward of Prospect Point (Observation Point pre-1900), some of the rocks and reefs that claimed the

143

Beaver still exist, though extensive dredging in this area has caused many to tumble down into the deeper water along with parts of the *Beaver*. Eastward of Prospect Point and where the south tower of Lion's Gate Bridge now stands was a nasty shoal of huge rocks, gravel and silt. As it receded toward what today is Lumberman's Arch, Parthia Shoal was formed reaching out to almost mid-channel before extending eastward to Brockton Point. Farther east of that hazard lay Burnaby Shoal, an unexpected outcrop of submerged granite that claimed many ships before having a white and red lighted sector beacon erected on it. When under the influence of the six- to eight-knot tidal currents that surged back and forth every six hours during those pre-dredged days, it became very difficult to navigate. When these conditions were coupled with darkness and fog, all but perhaps the most handy of vessel and knowing of masters, would prudently await the tidal slack to pass through.

Safe passage outbound through this narrows was from a point mid-channel off Brockton Point, with the ship's head on Prospect Point. This ensured a safe passage by Parthia and Calamity Shoals. Then at Lumberman's Arch/Calamity Shoal area, the ship's head was hauled starboard until it bore on the south edge of Capilano Shoal. When Prospect Point came abeam, the ship's head was hauled to port until Point Atkinson lay at least a point (11–12 degrees) on the starboard bow, thereby ensuring a safe passage between Capilano Shoal and the rocks lying west of Prospect Point. This zigzag coarse was often referred to as a dog's leg.

On an ebb tide from this 20-mile long inlet, the outflowing current followed much this same course, and this caused considerable back eddies, especially along the south shore west of Prospect Point. On a flood tide, as the sea rushed back in such as the *Beaver* encountered on her last night, a small (westbound) back eddy is set up along the south shores inside of Prospect Point, which could have been useful to the *Beaver* trying to get out of the Narrows. However, the outflow of the Capilano River is carried across the channel on a flood tide, hence the deposit of silt and debris at Lumberman's Arch/ Parthia Shoal areas. Thus, even today, when breasting the flood tide through this area a

144

mariner will experience a southerly set toward the south tower of Lion's Gate Bridge, and this action rapidly accelerates the closer this shore is carried aboard, i.e., the vessel nears this shore.

George Marchant was an experienced mariner who knew these tides well. If planning a turn around, he would have taken advantage of them not by any turn to port as some have suggested, but by a turn to starboard. Using the back eddy to carry his stern westward, the main stream would drive his head around to the eastward. The *Beaver* was less than 125 feet long after removal of her bowsprit, and the Narrows opened up at this point to more then two cables wide. Had he carried on for a few more minutes, he would have had almost half a mile, in which to turn. (In fact, I have turned the modern *Beaver* replica around at this very same place many times with no problem at all, using the tides the same way. I, of course, had the advantage of good visibility, twin screws, a well-dredged channel and good markers.) But according to George Marchant, none of these were present July 26, 1888.

Summer fog or heavy mist will often appear off the mouth of the Capilano River during July and August as the cold icy water runoff of the river meets the warmer salt waters flushing through the Narrows. As a boy, camping overnight at this area to fish, I would find a soft hollow of sand between the large rocks that radiated the heat gathered through the day, and bed down wrapped in an old Hudson Bay blanket, only to find myself well dampened next morning by the early morning fog. Captain Marchant may have entered such a fog while experiencing a southward set without comprehending his danger, which seems very unlikely.

Most mariners, before the advent of radar, used their whistle to get an echo off a nearby shore line in poor visibility; indeed, it was standard practice on this coast at least. Sound travels at 1,200 feet per second. Thus, a one-second whistle echo (i.e., a half second from the ship to the echo board, and a half second to return to the mariner's ear) indicated the echo board (i.e., shoreline) to be approximately 600 feet or one cable away from the whistle source. The high, steep rock cliff of Prospect Point makes an excellent echo board. Even without a whistle blast, the heavy slapping of the *Beaver*'s paddles striking the water should have echoed back a warning before she got into danger.

Whether Marchant was aware of any of this or not is unknown. Whether he attempted any maneuvers also seems blurred in retrospect. It would appear from the pictures we have that the *Beaver* drove up on the rocks on an angle while heading in a southwesterly direction shortly before high-water slack, and that the receding tide not only left the vessel firmly secured for the night, but also allowed her crew to climb down and wade safely ashore.

While engineer Evans mentions no engine movements, some must have taken place, if not before she hit, certainly immediately afterwards. If the engines had been coupled together, the cranks would be at ninety degrees to each other, thus presenting a good turning moment for the pistons to push them through their cycles and the *Beaver* could have stopped herself quite readily if her shoreward set had been realized in time. If she had not driven up on the rocks with a great deal of inertia behind her, the engines should have been able to slip her off again before the tide turned to ebb and she settled into her final resting place. However, if the engines had been running independently with the clutch disengaged, as would be the case during landing or departure, it could be possible for one of the cranks to stop on top or bottom dead centers and the push or pull of that piston unable to rotate that side of the paddlewheel shaft until the engine was pried or barred off dead centre. Whether that happened is not known, but if the engines were frantically rung astern as danger was realized and only the inboard or port engine answered, the ship would slew quickly to that side long before any way or forward motion was off her. As the coupling was found rusted in the open position, I believe that this was the way it was that fateful night in 1888, and with only the port engine going astern, the *Beaver* actually sheared out of control onto the rocks.

Neither Mister Crow-Baker or Saunders received word of the *Beaver*'s grounding until late the next day, as the mornings mail did not leave Vancouver until 10:00 A.M. By that time Captain Marchant, returning to the *Beaver* with hope of floating her off on top of the flood tide, found her flooded with only a portion of

146

her hull and deckhouse still above the surface. It became obvious, by the lead of the anchor chain, which had been dropped soon after she became stranded, that she had shifted and broke in a plank doing so.

She now had become a wreck, requiring expensive salvage to be removed. Neither Edgar Crow-Baker or Henry Saunders when they viewed her deemed her worthy of such cost, and advertised the old dowager for sale in a "where is, as is" condition. No offers were received, and each day as the tide surged in and out, her weary bones settled a little more firmly on the large sharp rocks at the foot of Lookout (Prospect) Point, that had claimed her.

Through the next four years that followed she became a curiosity visited by many. Some came to look, to sketch or to paint her; others lugged in cameras to take pictures for posterity. And many who came took away a small memento of the first great steamship to serve this coast. By 1892, denuded of much of her dignity and badges of honor with her hull covered in barnacles and open to the weather, she still boasted a tall funnel, a mast that stood proudly erect and a windowless wheelhouse watching all the new ships that passed her by.

But finally the end of her shame drew neigh. In early July, 1892, the log tow of the old steam tug *Pilot* brushed against her tired frames, carrying away her starboard wheel and box. Groaning like a weary soul possessed, her funnel crashed forward crushing her wheelhouse and toppling her mast, and she teetered reluctant to leave the world above the water. The *Pilot*, believe it or not, was under the command of the same man who had left the old *Beaver* in her precarious position five years earlier.

George Marchant is credited with pioneering the towing of log booms south through both Seymour Narrows and the Yuculta Rapids with the old *Beaver*. He also was master of the iron-hulled steam tug *Tepic* before commanding the *Pilot* and would go on as already noted, to sinking the brand new tug *Superior* in 1902. All together George Marchant would command more ships than any other master on this coast, at least within his lifetime, and sink or damage more than any other before passing peacefully away in his sleep in late 1925.

The *Beaver* teetered on her perch for a fortnight longer, until the large CPN paddlesteamer *Yosemite*, outbound at twelve-plus knots, threw her great wash ashore. Then, with a sigh of a departed soul, her boiler rolled out carrying away the port wheel and box, and the *Beaver* slid off her humiliating rocks to hide herself forever below the dark waters. Only her thirty-ton boiler and broken paddlewheel peeked above the surface once in a while during extreme low tides.

A great deal of controversy appears to exist over the exact events of that fateful night and those that followed. No one seemed concerned about the wreck or her removal and certainly less about the cause of it. Captain Marchant gave at least two different accounts, the last one shortly before he died in 1925 at the age of eighty. He stated they were trying to turn around when she hit and that he stood by the *Beaver* all night in a rowboat; an earlier version of his story stated the crew remained aboard, sleeping in their berths until low water when they waded ashore. In 1919 Captain Marchant to the *Harbour and Shipping News*, stated there was a thick fog that night and they had left at 1:00 A.M. to be over at Newcastle Island to take coal bunkers at 8:00 A.M. The ship sheared against the rocks, and the crew remained aboard until morning, then went ashore in a rowboat and walked back to Vancouver. This would seem most logical, as no roads existed in the area and thick forests of trees grew down to the water's edge, so low water would expose the beach and a reasonable route to travel.

In 1906 the first serious salvage of this pioneer steamer was carried out by Charles C. Pilkey. He raised the thirty-ton Spratt boiler and beached it at the north foot of Heatly Street, hoping to interest the city into buying it and placing it on display in the newly dedicated Stanley Park. Failing to get their interest, he moved it over to Cate's yard in North Vancouver then went back and salvaged one half of the paddlewheel shaft.

Failing any financial support in this country, he offered these salvaged artifacts to the Washington Historical Society. In 1909 it was moved to Tacoma where it was displayed along with an anchor found off Fort Nisqually, reported to be the *Beaver*'s from Captain McNeill's days.

148

It was unfortunate it could not be displayed in Canada. Luckily the good people in Washington realized its worth, and they saved this wonderful artifact until we Canadians could grow up and really appreciate how the *Beaver* created her legend. As a locally born Canadian, I'm glad we have people like Fred Rogers (1962) and Walter Rudek (1972), who salvaged the other paddle-wheel crankshaft, side lever and anchor, etc., from the depths of the *Beaver*'s final resting place. These items were donated to the Vancouver Maritime Museum, which I support in a small way and have served as director of for a short time. At least we can claim that much recognition of our historic marine past.

Finally, on a cold, spring day in 1992, *Beaver*'s old boiler was returned to Vancouver, and mounted for all to see at Vancouver Maritime Museum. For the dedication of this event, I took the replica SS *Beaver*, sparkling in fresh paint with all flags flying, and moored her in the small museum harbor while the speeches were read and our national anthem flowed forth from the loud speakers.

The *Beaver* legend really is alive, and all who know are proud to be part of it.

Epilogue

MOST SCHOOL STUDENTS IN BRITISH COLUMBIA, AT LEAST THOSE OF my era, were introduced to the Hudson's Bay Company's legendary brigantine-rigged, steam paddlewheel *Beaver*, through a few paragraphs in our history books and a quaint woodcut picture few of us had ever seen the like of. The little I did learn about her was quickly forgotten as I supplemented the family's lean income by going to sea at the tender age of sixteen, as the older more skilled seamen went to war or manned the ships carrying supplies across the U-boat threatened Atlantic. A dim recall of the foreboding dark countenance of James Douglas, the father of British Columbia, and a nagging knowledge that the *Beaver* had come to her end somewhere around Stanley Park sufficed to satisfy my historical roots until I became the father of two inquisitive growing boys.

One day we were lazing along under a light summer's breeze in the straits off Vancouver in our tiny sloop, when the strangest apparition climbed up from the horizon off our quarter and slowly converged. I rubbed my eyes with disbelief, there was no doubt in my mind that what I beheld paddling so serenely toward us was the reincarnation of that strange-looking ship of my school history books. She closed on a course for Vancouver, passing us less than ten cables off, the sedate "slap-slap" of her paddlewheels striking the water quite audible to our ears. I was so awestruck by what I saw and heard, that I had to pinch myself to prove I was not lost on the seas of 1836, where the HBC's *Beaver* reigned supreme on this lonely, oft-times hostile coast.

A few days later we drove to where she was berthed, and ventured aboard for a look around. Only then did I realize she was in fact a Royal Canadian Naval vessel manned by regular naval personnel. But only her light rigging and rather frail-looking paddlewheels caused me to doubt that she was anything else then a bonafide wooden sailing ship with steam-powered paddlewheels, until I reached her wooden lined hold where the sound of a diesel

150

engine pulsed through her bulkhead alerting me that she was in fact a sham—a very fascinating one, to be sure, but a sham nevertheless.

Little did I recognize then, that in my far-off retirement years I would realize the command of this fine *Beaver* replica. It was a command I held for almost ten years, and during which many passengers and visitors had inquired to her historic significance. Her appointment and upkeep were such that many believed they were actually aboard the original—that she was a wooden ship, a steamship, and that the paddlewheels actually propel us along!

During those wonderful years of command, my own knowledge of this replica and the original ship she commemorated grew extensively. I ventured here to share it with the reader. Hopefully my mariner's eyes and engineering knowledge provide a more interesting aspect from which to view the tumultuous events experienced by the *Beaver* and her people, as they transformed this unwanted land into the opulent jewel of John A. Macdonald's necklace of confederation.

The Royal Canadian Navy's replica of the *Beaver* came into being seventy-two years after the original slid below the water off Prospect Point. She had been the former ammunition tender Y.S.F. 216, built to the Royal Canadian Navy's high standards for vessels in this trade by Allied Shipyards in 1957. In 1965, Canada's century of confederation (1867 1967) loomed ahead, as did the centennial of the union of Vancouver Island and the Mainland (1866 1966) and, five years later, the century mark (1871 1971) since British Columbia became the confederation's sixth province making Canada a nation, sea-to-sea. Great plans were envisioned for an appropriate way in which to commemorate these important anniversaries. Many wonderful events were considered, and those that finally were realized gave great satisfaction to their planners and expediters—few more so than the creation of a full-sized replica of the Hudson's Bay Company's pioneer paddlewheel steamer *Beaver*.

Funding for this project was very limited due to its belated selection. Fortunately, the Royal Canadian Navy was able to donate a suitable vessel, and then most generously offered to complete the project as their contribution to Canada's centennial.

Their designers and engineers completed the drawings and specifications in very short order. Commander William E. (then Lieutenant) "Dusty" Rhodes was placed as coordinator of the project. Working within the dockyard, he organized the labor, material and modifications to have the replica ready by the spring of 1966.

The navy's fleet school instructors set their students to work building many of the required components such as capstans, cannons, spars and rigging, etc., as classroom projects. The timber for the masts and spars were donated in the round and hewed into shape by the students and instructors, but the bulk of the main work such as the wooden overlay, the setting up of the gear and rigging, and the relocation and overhaul of equipment and machinery was carried out at the dockyard where Frank DeGruchy was lead hand in the shipwright's shop.

The naval dockyard at Esquimalt has undergone many changes through the years since the Royal Navy dedicated it as their western base in 1852. The Public Works Department, not the Navy, operated the original graving dock opened in 1884 by HMS Cormorant. This set the style for West Coast management even before the First World War when Canada created the Royal Canadian Navy around such old veterans as the *Rainbow*, *Givinchy* and *Naden*. Civilians carried out the trades, while the navy supervised and manned the ships. The SS *Beaver* was born at this old dock, which had spent most of the years since 1926 as a mooring basin for smaller naval vessels. And when it was reactivated as a graving dock and christened Naden in 1971, the SS *Beaver* in all her glory, bedecked in flags officiated for the dedication.

Little exists today to show us what the original *Beaver* actually looked like, though some sketches done during her earlier years have survived. People of the Hudson's Bay Company were dedicated recordkeepers, but two wars that saw London bombed, and a final move of all company records to Canada thereafter, has realized some loss. Thus, the building of the *Beaver* replica largely depended for guidance on reproduced drawing created by the United States Department of Interior and those drawings produced by the ship repair yards in Victoria during the years 1845

152

to 1889 who had been entrusted with her repair and upkeep. In addition, there are early glass negative plate photographs that have survived from the same period.

From this information, the Royal Canadian Navy did a marvelous job, creating a replica of almost identical proportions, displacement and aspect. While built with a very limited budget that necessitated a great deal of improvisation to realize, she was only expected to serve within sheltered waters for five short years. That the ship has survived to this present time must give great satisfaction to all who have served her and much historic understanding to those who take the opportunity sail on her.

The selection of the YSF type of ship is possibly the vital key to the longevity of the SS *Beaver*. Her strong frame and plating have not tired of carrying the huge burden of wood overlay nor the thousands of pounds of lead ballast to steady her ungainly top hamper. The YSF hull form provides good maneuverability with minimum power requirements, and her original navy-specified diesel engines continue to spin her heavy propellers in a most comforting manner. With full flooding and pumping capability to each of her six watertight compartments, a beam of just less than forty feet at her sponson deck, and twin rudders controlled from two hydraulic steering stations, the navy's YSF is like the noble donkey of yore, completely hidden beneath its 140-foot-long over burden.

Christened the SS *Beaver* in a formal naval ceremony in 1966, she sailed that summer under command of Lt. Ian Sturgess and visited several ports in the Strait of Georgia and Puget Sound. They carried a navy crew dressed in period costumes, the *Beaver* flew the Hudson's Bay Company flag of that era, and with the help of local actors they enacted several important events in our country's history.

In 1967, with Lieutenant Robert McIlwaine as executive officer and a crew of eight seamen, the SS *Beaver* departed Fort Nisqually (Tacoma) in Puget Sound, and sailed north to Fort Simpson, stopping overnight at such out of the way places as the friendly Indian village in Hartly Bay. For the next three years the *Beaver* remained berthed at Esquimalt, before again showing the flag on a cruise of British Columbia ports. This time she was under command of Lt. J. Gracy to commemorate B.C. joining John A.'s confederation.

In 1972, the municipality of Fort Langley, having restored the old Hudson's Bay fort at this historical site and built an impressive museum nearby, bought the SS *Beaver*. They planned to berth her on the Fraser River, where people visiting their fort and museum could board and explore her. Unfortunately, the cost of realizing this caused them to rethink their plans and they sold the ship to Doug Emery who proposed to fit her out for charter cruising. Captain Dennis P. Farina sailed her over to Vancouver where she endeavored to earn her way in the harbor cruising business.

When Doug Emery died suddenly in a car accident, his partner Jim Byrne of Gulf of Georgia Towing sold the ship to Peter Douglas who attempted to make it a paying proposition. When he failed, Barry M. Graham bought her and made the most valued contribution to the SS *Beaver*, by building a large main deck cabin forward of her funnel and a disco lounge in her hold. The SS *Beaver* then took on the appearance of the original in 1864, when the Royal Navy chartered her for a hydrographic ship and put Lt. Daniel Pender (Pender Island) in charge.

Barry Graham leased the ship to Colleen Whitney, and she incorporated the *Beaver* Steamship Company to manage its affairs. Bill Yates joined her as a partner, and Captain Cyril Andrews became master of the vessel. Together, this threesome pampered their passengers with comfort and entertainment. And these satisfied patrons, after a memorable trip on this unique ship, became her best goodwill emissaries.

Colleen invited not only travel agents, but also government tourist and political figures on complimentary cruises. She had a costumed Captain Hudson hand out special two-for-one cruise offers at street corners and at tourist conventions, and advertised heavily through the media. But there were a couple of problems, and these finally drove the aging replica into a backwater morass. First, the ship was not brought up to Ministry of Transportation standards for a passenger vessel, and had to sail as a charter yacht. Second, the city preempted her commercial berth, and the cost of yacht berthing prohibited the *Beaver* realizing a profit position during the short B.C. summer season. The *Beaver* lay for three long years exposed to wind and rain while her bones rusted and her wooden overlay rotted, before a young man with a dream in his heart took up her cause.

With the staunch support of his lovely wife Sheri, Don Christie begged and borrowed from family and friends enough money to buy the ship and he began refitting her for a passenger vessel in the coming Expo 86 tourist trade. He invited me to join her as mate and relief master, and I worked along with his large group of volunteers to rebuild her into a Class Four Passenger Vessel.

Due to medical problems, Captain Cy Andrews was forced to relinquish command and I took over. With my son Rod, sailing as second engineer, we loaded 100 passengers at Coal Harbor and sailed to Expo 86. I made more than 1,000 voyages with this ship, yet I always puffed up with pride when our passengers took a moment before going ashore, to accord us accolades for a happy cruise.

After completing voyage # 1,267 New Years day morning in 1996, I settled in for a long winter's nap, assured the *Beaver* would not be wanted before the spring sunshine returned to our coast. It was snowing and dark when her manager next phoned me. The *Beaver* had been sold and her new owner wanted her over in Victoria. It was early March and I was not enthused. I used every dodge my desperate gray cells could dredge up, but to no avail. We had to sail that night to honor the delivery date and receive payment.

It was 2:00 a.m. when my wife Patricia and I climbed aboard. Our chief engineer Tony had everything warmed up, including a lovely pot of coffee. The manager and the new skipper from Victoria had just arrived, so we slipped our lines and ghosted over to a fuel barge to take on bunkers. Our departure was timed for the tide at Active Pass, and by 3:00 a.m. we had been cleared by traffic and were outward bound through the Narrows. However, all was not well.

The *Beaver* sensed we were taking her away from her beloved home waters, and developed an ornery streak that could not be placated. I have always enjoyed a special tolerance from this strange little ship; she sort of liked me, just as I admired her. Where other mariners cried and cursed as they tried to maneuver her, she seemed almost to do the right thing without much input from me. I felt blessed with her ability to make me look good! However, this was not the case that cold, snowy morning in March when we sailed away for the last time.

It took all my dexterity to keep her under control as we pushed up against the incoming flood tide, and I was quite warm and quite tired when Capilano Light finally slid astern. With the separation buoy blinking ahead and the horizon beginning to clear, I invited James,the new skipper, to take over the helm while Patricia and I went below for a hot coffee and Danish. Fifteen or twenty minutes later, rested and my good humor restored, I left Pat with Tony and the manager, while I went back up to the wheelhouse to see how James was making out.

I was not surprised at what I found, having during my coffee break seen lights outside the main lounge cabin windows going about in the strangest way. The wheelhouse doors were wide open, charts were scattered on the chart table, and both the radar and the compass light were turned on full. James had the look and the stance of a wild man. I knew better than to see humor in his situation, so swiftly using the radar as a pointer system, I checked the wildly careening ship and steadied her north of the flashing red bell buoy, while James stuttered and stammered trying to explain what had gone wrong.

A slow compass and double reflection through her many-windowed wheelhouse caused dark or foggy piloting to be confusing, Fortunately, the radar could be used to double check this and even assist when one's eyes were bedeviled by the reflected lights. We were an hour late on the tide because of her tardy progress, but as soon as she felt the ebb tide under her keel, the foolishness stopped and we made a record run to Victoria. We even had to wait for the fireboat that was to lead us into harbor and around James Bay.

Today, as the SS *Beaver* still attempts to relive the era of her namesake, with lofty spars, waving flags and slapping paddle-wheels through the waters that once breasted Fort Victoria, nothing can really depict the austere and often harsh conditions expe-

156

rienced by both the ship's crew and those who sailed in her on HBC business. Hopefully, my story has given a greater appreciation of the difficulties those pioneers surmounted to forge the comforts and circumstance sometimes taken for granted in this era of bountiful returns.

Take a moment to consider this little vessel, and see her not as a strange-looking steamship, but as a bridge carrying us over from the age of muscle power to the age of thermal dynamics, miracle metals and electronic wizardry.

Beaver Masters
[1834 – 1888]

Capt. D. Home	1834 – 1836
Capt. W. McNeill	1836 – 1841
Capt. W. Brotchie	1842 – 1843
Capt. D. Duncan	1843 – 1844
Capt. C. Humphreys	1844 – 1845
Capt. C. Dodd	1845 – 1851
Capt. W. Stuart	1851 – 1852
Capt. C. Dodd	1852 – 1856
Capt. J. Swanson	1856 – 1858
Capt. J.L. Sinclair	1858 – 1859
Capt. H.G. Lewis	1859 – 1860
Lt. D.R. Pender (R.N.)	1862 – 1872
Capt. G. Rudlin	1872 – 1874
Capt. T. Pamphlet	1874 – 1875
Capt. W. Mitchell	1875 – 1876
Capt. J.D. Warren	1876 – 1878
Capt. J.F. Jager	1979 – 1882
Capt. G. Marchant	1883 – 1888

Bibliography

Berton, Pierre. *The Arctic Grail* McClelland and Stewart, Toronto, 1988.

Berton, Pierre. *The Great Railway* McClelland and Stewart, Toronto, 1972.

Denison, Merrill. *The Barley and The Stream* McClelland and Stewart, Toronto, 1955.

Drushka, Ken. *Against Wind and Weather* Douglas & McIntyre, Vancouver, 1981.

Greene, Ruth. *Personality Ships of British Columbia* Marine Tapestry Publications Ltd., 1969.

Hacking, Norman R. & W. Kaye Lamb. *The Princess Story* Mitchell Press, Vancouver, 1974.

Harris, Stephen L. *Fire and Ice* Pacific Search Press, Seattle, 1976.

Hull, Soules & Soules. *Vancouver's Past* Gordon Soules Publishing, Vancouver, 1974.

McCann , Leonard G. *The Honourable Company's Beaver* Friesen/Vancouver Maritime Museum,1980.

Middleton, Lynn. *Place Names of the Pacific Northwest Coast* Evergreen Press, Vancouver, 1969.

Nicholson, George. *Vancouver Island's West Coast* Morriss Co., Victoria, 1962.

Ormsby, Margaret A. *British Columbia: A History* MacMillan of Canada, Toronto, 1956.

Pethick, Derek. *S.S. Beaver: The ship that saved the West* Mitchell Press Ltd., Vancouver, 1970.

Rogers, Fred. *Shipwrecks of British Columbia* J. J. Douglas Ltd., 1976.

Index

ABBYSSINIA, CPR Orient line, 140
ACTIVE, Hastings Mill Tug, 130
Alaska, U.S.A., 8, 10
Albion Iron Works (V.M.D.) B.C.,
    22, 117, 123
Alexandria, B.C., 45
ALICE, iron-hulled schooner, 60
Allied Shipyard, 151
Amelia Island (named for Lady
    Douglas), 107
Amundsen, Roald, 59
Anderson, A. C. (Lillooet gold trail),
    91
Anderson Lake, B.C. (1858–59,
    named after gold trail builder),
    48, 91
Andrews, Captain Cyril, 154
ARCHIMEDES, bark, 60
Archimedes, (Greek mathematician
    /inventor), 58
Arthur, Peter (*BEAVER* engineer),
    19, 56
Astor, John Jacob, 8
Astrolabe (cross-staff/sextant), 103
ATAHUALPA, U.S. bark, 24
Ayrshire, Scotland, 46
Baker, Edgar Crow, 134
Banfield, B.C., 133
Barkley, Capt. C. W., 103
Barkley Sound, B.C., 103
Barker, William, Barkerville miner,
    94
Barkerville, B.C., 94
Bayley, George, 54
Beaver Bay, (Port McNeil area)
    B.C., 32
BEAVER's boilers 1867, 109, 115,
    124, 142
BEAVER, HBC steamer 6, 8, 13, 43

61, 97, 117, 141
Beaver Rock, Discovery Pass., 133
Beaver House, 9
BEAVER, SS (Replica), 152
Begbie, Judge Mathew Baillie, 90,
    93
Bella Bella, B.C., 26, 108
BELLE, Hasting's Mill tug, 140
Bentinck Arm, B.C., 26, 108
Bessemer, Sir Henry (1861), 111
Big Bend Trail, B.C., 8, 12
Birmingham Public Libraries, 109
BLACK DIAMOND, coal steamer,
    120
Black Douglas (Sir James's father),
    34
Blackwall, Thames, 14
Blanshard, Governor Richard (V.I.),
    48
Bolduc, Father (Cowlitz Mission), 17
Boulton, John, 14
Boulton & Watt, 14, 56, 109
BOXER, HMS (RN), 123
Brew, Chartres (B.C. police), 90
Brewer, Rev. H.B., 17
Brighouse, Sam, 136
British Columbia, 6, 10, 22, 93
Centennial, (B.C. joins Confeder-
    ation 1871–1971), 151
British Columbia & Victoria Steam
    Navigation Co., 97
BC Towing & Transportation Co.,
    120, 134
Brotchie, Capt. (*BEAVER*), 44
Bute Inlet, B.C., 38, 108, 118
Byrne, Jim (G of G), 154
CADBORA, HBC schooner, 31, 49,
    59
Camel Floats (salvage equip.), 134

160

Camosack (Victoria), B.C., 40
Canada, Dominion of, 6
Canada's Century of Confederation
   (1867–1967), 151
Canadian Pacific Navigation Co.,
   97, 122
Canadian Pacific Railways Ltd., 6,
   122, 134
Cape Flattery, Wash., U.S.A., 10, 59
Cape Horn, S.A., 15, 50
Cape Mudge (Campbell River),
   B.C., 60
Cape Reyes, California, 96
Cape Scott, B.C., 28
Cariboo, B.C., 94, 112
Carless, (*BEAVER* engineer), 56
Carnarvon, Lord, 119
Cascade Mountains (Fire Moun-
   tains), 17
Cast Iron, (creating it), 110
Charles II, HRH, King of England,
   7
Chief Che-wech-i-kan (Coal Tyee),
   49
China, 132
Christie, Don and Sheri (SS
   Beaver), 154
CIRCUS, schooner, 120
CITY of PANAMA, steamer, 133
Clayquot Sound, Vancouver Island,
   B.C., 60
CLEARMONT, Fulton's first steam-
   boat, 113
Coal Tyee (Chief Che-wech-i-kan),
   46
Coltman, Edwin, 118
COLUMBIA, HBC bark, 15, 23, 31
Columbia River, Wash., 8, 63
Colvilletown (Nanaimo, B.C.), 49
COMMODORE, Pacific Mail
   steamer, 63
Cook, Capt. George, 7, 24
CORMORANT, HMS (1884), 152
Cort, Henry (1784), 111
COUNTESS of DUFFERIN (CPR

locomotive #374), 139
Cowichan Bay, B.C., 29, 61
COWLITZ, HBC vessel, 44
Cowlitz River/Valley, Wash., 17, 33
Crow-Baker, Edgar, 134
Cutler, Lyman, 96
Darby, Capt.,16
DeGruchy, Frank, 152
Desolation Sound (Powell River
   area), 108
Dewdney Trail, B.C. (HBC), 12,
   48, 63, 90
Dewdney Trunk Road, 90
DIANA, (PMC-Chinese steam
   launch), 132
DISCOVERY, schooner, 120
Dixon, Capt., 103
Dixon Entrance, B.C., 103
Dodd, Capt. Charles (*BEAVER*), 16,
   44, 60, 95
Dodd's Narrows (Nanaimo, B.C.)
   named after Capt. C. Dodd, 108,
   125
Douglas, Mrs. Amelia (née
   Conolly), 34
Douglas Channel (named for Sir
   James), B.C., 107
Douglas, Sir James (Governor HBC
   /B.C.), 22, 34, 49, 61, 99, 131
Douglas, Peter, 154
DRYAD, HBC vessel, 26
Duncan, Capt. Alexander
   (*BEAVER*), 44
Dunn, John, 23
DUNSMUIR, lumber ship, 139
Dunsmuir, Joan (Robert's wife), 46
Dunsmuir, Robert (coal baron), 32,
   44, 46, 49, 118, 134
East India Co., 42
Ebey, Col. I. N., U.S. Army, 95, 96
Emery, Doug, 154
EMMA, whaling steamer, 120
ENTERPRISE, HBC steamer, 97
Esquimalt, B.C. (RN base), 39, 45,
   48, 95

Esquimalt & Nanaimo Railway, 118, 134
ETTA WHITE, steam tug, 121, 132
Evans, W.H. (BEAVER), 142
Everest (surveyor of India), 104
Everett, Wash., 138
Farina, Capt. Dennis P., 154
Finlayson, Duncan (HBC), 23
Fitzhugh Sound, B.C., 99
Flemming, Ian (CPR), 138
Fort Astoria, Columbia River, U.S.A., 8
Fort Atabaska, Alta., 12
Fort Colville, Wash, 12, 48, 63
Fort Fraser, Nechako River, B.C., 7
Fort Garry, Winnipeg, Man., 12, 40
Fort George (Prince George), B.C., 7
Fort George (Columbia River, formerly Ft. Astoria), 8, 33
Fort Hope, B.C., 11, 48, 63, 91
Fort Kamloops (Thompson River), B.C., 11, 45, 63
Fort Langley (Fraser River), B.C., 11, 12, 28
Fort McLeod, Hart Hwy., B.C., 7
Fort McLoughlin (Bella Bella), B.C., 26, 32
Fort Nisqually (Tacoma), Wash., 13, 16, 32, 153
Fort Rupert (Port McNeil), Vancouver Island, B.C., 30, 33, 46
Fort Simpson (Prince Rupert area), B.C., 13, 26, 32, 109
Fort Stikine, Alaska, 33, 45
Fort St. James, Stuart Lake, B.C., 7
Fort Steele,(NWMP) Kootney River, B.C., 89
Fort Taku, Alaska, 41, 45
Fort Vancouver, Columbia River, USA, 8, 10, 16, 32
Fort Victoria (now Victoria, capital of B.C.), 33, 46, 58, 63
Fort Yale (lower Fraser River), B.C., 11, 91, 119, 135
FORWARD, HMS (RN), 109
FRAM, Amundsen's ship, 59
Fraser River, 11, 120
Fraser, Simon, 6, 24
Fullerton, John (Beaver), 125
Fulton, Robert (CLERMONT,1807), 113
Galiano, Com. D. A. (Spain), 103
Gallows Point, Nanaimo, B.C., 62
Gardener, Capt., 132
Gardener, Dr. Meredith (Mount St. Helens), 17
Garrett, Richard, 113
GEORGIANA, HBC vessel, 61
GIVINCHY, HMCS (RCN), 152
Gladstone, Wm. E., prime minister of England, 90
GLENORA, river steamer, 136
GONDOLIER, ship, 133
Gore, Lloyd, 140
GOVERNOR DOUGLAS, (first steamer built in B.C., 1858), 92, 97
Gracy, Lt. J. (RCN-1971), 154
Graham, Barry M., 154
Grahame, C. HBC factor, 109
Grant, Capt. William (sealing/whaling, Victoria), 123
Grant, Walter Colquhoun, 48
Granville (Vancouver), B.C., 119, 137
GRAPPLER, HMS (RN sloop), 98, 108, 120
Gray, Judge, 133
Great Northern R.R.,138
Greenwich, England (zero longitude), 99, 104
Green, Wigran & Green, (London, England), 14, 58
Greer's Beach, Vancouver, B.C., 137
Hagelund, Rod., 155
Haidas, Queen Charlotte Island tribe, 63

162

Hailstone, W., 136
Hall, Joseph (1816), 111
Hamilton, 16
HARO, Hastings tug, 130
Harrison, William, 118
Hastings Mill, Vancouver, 134
HECATE, HMS (RN), 98,
Helen Point, Active Pass, 107
Helmcken, Dr. John S., 26
HENRY BUCK, (rammed
    BEAVER), 125
Hill, J. J. (GNRR), 138
Home Bay, Princess Royal Island
    (named for Capt D. Home),107
Home, Capt. David (BEAVER), 15,
    19, 24, 29, 38
Hood Point, Howe Sound, 107
Hoonah, Alaskan Indian village, 96
Horse Power, capstan, 110
Hudson's Bay Company, 6, 16, 48
Hudson, Capt. Henry, 7
Humphrey, Capt. Charles (*BEAVER*),
    44
Irving, Capt. John, CPN (son of
    William), 121
Irving, Capt. William (Pioneer
    Steamboat Line), 97, 121
ISAAC TODD, English troop ship, 8
ISABEL, Stamp's tug (1866), 132
Jagers, Capt. J. F. (*BEAVER*), 133
James Bay, Victoria, B.C., 119
Jasper House, Alta., 12
Johnson, Tom, 25
Johnstone Straits, B.C., 38, 108
Juan Fernandez Island, Chile, 15
JULIA BARCLAY, U.S. steamer, 97
Kanakas (Sandwich Islanders), 24,
    94
Kane, Paul (painter of Mount St.
    Helens 1847), 18
Kensington Museum, England, 58
Kilcat, Indian village, B.C., 25
Klondike, Yukon (gold rush), 26
Knight Inlet, B.C., 38
Kootenay Valley, 8

Kupreanof Island, Alaska, 95
LaBOUCHERE, HBC steamer, 95
LAMA, (J. J. Astor's) brig, 29, 33
Lander, Judge, U.S.A., 62
Leschi, Nisqually Indian Chief,
    U.S.A., 62
Lewis, Capt. Herbert, 109
Lillooet, B.C., 11, 91
Locomotive Boiler, 114
LONDON, brig, 120
LORNE (Dunsmuir's steam tug),
    122
Loughborough Inlet, B.C., 38
Lytton, Sir Edward. B., 90
Macdonald, Prime Minister, Sir.
    John A., 116, 118, 151
Mackenzie, Alexander, NWT Co., 7,
    24, 2,
McKay, Joseph W., 49
McKay Point, New Castle Island
    (named after J. W. McKay),107
MacLean, Mayor M. A.
    (Vancouver), 137
McCann, Leonard G., VMM, 109
McIlwaine, Lt. Robert (RCN-1967),
    153
McLoughlin, Dr. John, 18, 23, 61
McLoughlin Point, Victoria, 107
McMillan Island (Fraser River/
    Langley), 29
McNeill, Capt. Wm. H., 30, 33, 57
Maalaca Bay, Lahaina, 41
Madigan, Benjamin (*BEAVER* engi-
    neer), 125
Malcolm Island, B.C., 28
Maloney, Capt., U.S. Army, 62
Marchant, Capt. George, 71, 108,
    134
Marchant Rock, Estevan Point
    (Vancouver Island), 108
Mare Island, USN, Calif., 63
MARY DARE, schooner, 59
MAUDE, Spratt's first steamer
    (1872), 123
Maudslay Sons & Field, Lambeth,

163

56, 58
Mears, Capt. John, 8, 103
MEG MERRILEES, schooner, 131
Mercator, Gerardus (projected sphere onto flat chart), 100
Milbanke Sound, B.C., 24
Millar, Capt. (OTTER), 60
Mitchell Inlet (Queen Charlotte Islands), B.C., 61
Moberly, Alan, 119
Monterey, California (1845), 49
Montreal, Que., 7
Moody, Col., Royal Engineers, 95
Moody, Sewell Prescott (Pioneer Mills), 132
Morton, Charles, 118
Mouat, Capt. W.A., 96
Mount St. Helens, 17
Muir John (Colvilletown), 49
NADEN, HMCS (RCN), 152
Nahwitti (Indian village), B.C., 33, 44
Nanaimo, B.C. (Naymo/Ninimo, 1851–52), 18, 49, 59, 62
Nasmyth, James (Carron Iron Works), 113
Nass River, B.C., 26, 35
Nekwilta Inlet, B.C., 99
NEREIDE, HBC bark, 29, 43
Newcomen, engineer, 14, 19
New Caledonia (B.C.) 6, 11, 15, 60
New Westminster (pioneer capital of B.C.), 89, 118
Nootka Sound (Vancouver Island), B.C., 24, 103
Norfolk Public School, Victoria, 109
North West Trading Co., 7, 8
Observatory Inlet, Anyox, B.C., 104
Ogden, Peter S., 26, 41
Okanagan Valley, 8
Onderdonk, Andrew, 120, 134
Oppenheiner, David and Isaac, 137
OTTER, HBC steamer, 50, 58, 63
Pacific Fur Co. (John Jacob Astor), 8
Pacific Mail Steamship Co., 45, 90,

132
Pamphlet, Capt. Tom (BEAVER), 131
Parker, Capt. (bark LORD WESTON), 60
Parrish, Father J. L. (Mount St. Helens), 17
Pearks, George, Crown Solicitor,93
Pemberton, Col. J. D., 59
Pend d'Oreille River, Wash., 63
Pender, Lt. Daniel (RN), 98, 121, 135, 154
Pig Iron (cast iron), 111
Pig War of 1859, 97
Pilkey, Charles C., 148
PILOT, salvage tug, 134, 147
Pioneer Steamboat Line, 122
PLUMPER, HMS (RN), 98
Point Ellice Bridge (collapsed May Day 1896), 123
Polaris (North Star),103
Port Douglas, B.C., 91
Port McNeil, Vancouver Island, 30
Port Moody, B.C., 119, 134, 136
Port Townsend, Wash., 60, 89
Powell, Dr. John, 137
Prince George, B.C., 11
Prince Rupert, B.C., 11, 26
PRINCESS ROYAL, HBC bark, 95
Prospect Point, Vancouver, B.C., 6, 10
Puget Sound Agricultural Co. (HBC), 45
Puget Sound, Wash., 28, 34
Puyallup, Indian reservation, Wash., 62
QUEEN, Hastings tug, 130
Queen Charlotte Islands, B.C., 61, 108
Queen Charlotte Sound, B.C., 99
Quesnel Forks, B.C., 94
RAINBOW, HMCS, 152
Rastic, James (1822), 111
RECOVERY, HBC sloop, 60, 61
Red River, Man., 7, 32, 40

RELIANCE, river steamer, 136
Rhodes, Lt. Wm. E. (RCN), 152
Richards, Capt. G. H. (RN), 97, 104
Rithet, R. P., 134
Robson, John, 137
Rogers, Fred, 149
Rogers, Jeremiah (Jericho/Point
  Grey), 132
ROCKET, Stephenson's locomotive,
  14
Royal Canadian Navy, 150
ROYAL CITY, river steamer, 136,
Royal Navy, 42, 48, 97
Royal Roads, Vancouver Island
  (Albert Head area), 130
ROYAL WILLIAM, steamship, 47
Roys, Capt. Thomas Welcome, 117,
  120
Rudek, Walter, 149
Rudlin, Captain George, 118, 120
Russians, Alaska, 8, 13, 26
Sandwich Islands (Hawaii), 15, 24,
  33
San Francisco, California, 50, 64, 96
Sangster, Capt. John, 96
Sapperton, B.C., 95
SATELLITE, HMS (RN), 93
Saunders, Harry, 110, 118, 120, 134
Safety Cove, Calvert Island, B.C.,
  99
SEA BIRD, Pacific Mail steamer, 90
SEA LION, Y & G steam tug, 130
Seattle, Wash., 122
Seymour, Gov. F., 107
Seymour Inlet (north of Port Hardy),
  B.C., 108
Seymour Narrows (Ripple Rock),
  B.C., 38, 118
Simpson, Governor George (HBC),
  9, 12, 23, 31, 131
Skeena River, B.C., 3
Skidegate Channel, B.C., 108
Skunk Cove, pilot station, 133
Smith, Donald, 138
Smith, Marcus (surveyor), 118

Smithe, William, B.C. premier, 136
Sooke, B.C., 39
South Pacific Co., 42
Southern Pacific RR, 50, 138
Spratt, Capt. Joe (Albion Iron
  Works), 22, 56, 117, 121
Sproat, Gilbert (Sproat Lake, Port
  Alberni), 131
Stafford, John, 118
Stamp, Capt. Edward (Hastings
  Mill), 131
Steel, (manufacturing), 111
Stevens, George, 138
Stephenson, George, 14, 114
Stikine River, Alaska, 13, 26, 96
Straits of Georgia, 29
Stuart, Capt. Charles E. (*BEAVER*),
  44
Sturgess, Lt. I. (RCN, 1966), 153
SUPERIOR, steam tug, 140
SURPRISE, Pacific Mail steamer, 90
SUTLEJ, HMS (RN),198
Swanson, Capt. John
  (*BEAVER/OTTER*), 60, 95
Symington, Angus, 113
Tacoma, Wash., 13
Tatoosh, Wash. (Juan de Fuca), 59
TEPIC, steel-hulled French tug, 147
Texada Island, B.C., 99
THETIS, HMS (RN), 61
Thompson, David, 8
Thompson River, (Kamloops) B.C.,
  11, 63
Thorne, (*BEAVER* engineer),58, 60
Titcomb, Capt., 132
Tlingit, Alaskan Indian tribe, 95, 96
Tolmie, Dr. John, 26, 62
TONQUIN, U.S. bark, 24
TRANSPORT (Spratt salvaged
  engines and boiler), 123
TRIBUNE, HMS (RN), 108
TRINCOMALEE, HMS (RN), 62
Trivett, Capt. J. F., 95
UMATILLA, Pacific Mail steamer,
  91

UNA, HBC vessel, 61,
UNION (scow built steamer), 125, 135
Valdez, Capt. C. (Spain), 103
VALLEYFIELD, HBC brig, 57
Vancouver, B.C., 6, 109, 139
Vancouver, Capt. George, 39, 99, 104
Vancouver Island, 27, 38, 47
Vancouver Maritime Museum, 22, 56, 109, 149
Van Horne, William C. (CPR), 136
Vermilion Pass, 8, 12
Victoria, B.C., 22, 39, 156
Victoria Colonist, newspaper, 126
Victoria, HRH, Queen, 35
Victoria Machinery Depot, 117
VICTORIA, army supply ship, 120
Victoria Whaling Adventurers Club, 117
Waddington, Alfred (surveyor), 118
Walla Walla, Wash., 48
War of 1812, 8, 23, 45
Warren, Capt. Art, 125
Warren, Capt. James D. (*BEAVER*), 125
Washington Historical Society, 148

Watt, Sir James, 14, 19, 111
Wellington (Dunsmuir's coal), B.C., 46, 49
WELLINGTON (large coal bark), 125
Whatcom (Bellingham) Wash., 89
Whitney, Coleen, 154
WILLIAM and ANN, HBC brig, 26
William 1st, Emperor of Germany, 123
Williams, Frank, 118
Williams, Thomas, 62
Winnipeg, Man., 12, 40
Winsby, Elizabeth. (Daughter of H. Saunders, BCTTC), 126
Work, John (HBC factor), 43, 61
Wrangle, Alaska, 26
Wrangle, Baron (Russian), 45
Wrought Iron, (creating), 110
XY Company, 7
Yale No.1, locomotive, 136
Yale Road (Emery Creek), 90
Yates, Wm., 154
Yellowhead Pass, (Kamloops, 11
YOSEMITE, CPN steamer, 56, 148
ZEALOUS, HMS (RN), 135

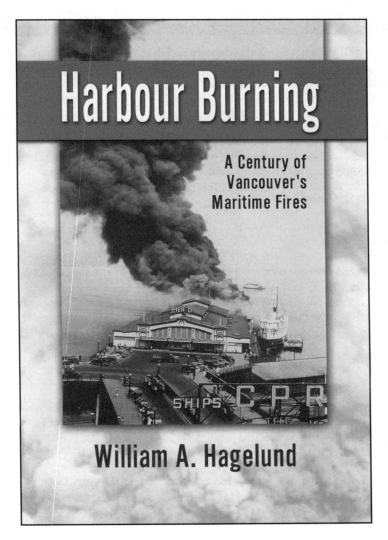

Harbour Burning

William A. Hagelund
ISBN 0-88839-488-8
5.5" x 8.5" • sc • 208 pages

More Great HANCOCK HOUSE History Titles

Big Timber Big Men
Carol Lind
ISBN 0-88839-020-3
8.5 x 11 • hc • 153 pp.

Border Bank Bandits
Frank Anderson
ISBN 0-88839-255-9
5.5 x 8.5 • sc • 88 pp.

B.C.'s Own Railroad
Lorraine Harris
ISBN 0-88839-125-0
5.5 x 8.5 • sc • 64 pp.

Buckskins, Blades, and Biscuits
Allen Kent Johnston
ISBN 0-88839-363-6
5.5 x 8.5 • sc • 176 pp.

Buffalo People
Mildred Valley Thornton
ISBN 0-88839-479-9
5.5 x 8.5 • sc • 208 pp.

Captain McNeill and His Wife the Nishga Chief
Robin Percival Smith
ISBN 0-88839-472-1
5.5 x 8.5 • sc • 256 pp.

Crooked River Rats
Bernard McKay
ISBN 0-88839-451-9
5.5 x 8.5 • sc • 176 pp.

End of Custer
Dale Schoenberger
ISBN 0-88839-288-5
5.5 x 8.5 • sc • 336 pp.

Gold Creeks & Ghost Towns (WA)
Bill Barlee
ISBN 0-88839-452-7
8.5 x 11 • sc • 224 pp.

Gold Creeks & Ghost Towns
Bill Barlee
ISBN 0-88839-988-X
8.5 x 11 • sc • 192 pp.

Gold! Gold!
Joseph Petralia
ISBN 0-88839-118-8
5.5 x 8.5 • sc • 112 pp.

Great Western Train Robberies
Don DeNevi
ISBN 0-88839-287-7
5.5 x 8.5 • sc • 202 pp.

Jailbirds & Stool Pigeons
Norman Davis
ISBN 0-88839-431-4
5.5 x 8.5 • sc • 144 pp.

Mackenzie Yesterday & Beyond
Alfred Aquilina
ISBN 0-88839-083-1
5.5 x 8.5 • sc • 202 pp.

Old Wooden Buildings
Donovan Clemson
ISBN 0-919654-90-8
8.5 x 11 • sc • 93 pp.

Plundertown, USA: Coos Bay Enters the Global Economy
Al Sandine
ISBN 0-88839-525-6
5.5 x 8.5 • sc • 176 pp.

Quest for Empire
Kyra Wayne
ISBN 0-88839-191-9
5.5 x 8.5 • sc • 415 pp.

Walhachin
Joan Weir
ISBN 0-88839-982-0
5.5 x 8.5 • sc • 104 pp.

Walter Moberly and the Northwest Passage by Rail
Daphne Sleigh
ISBN 0-88839-510-8
5.5 x 8.5 • sc • 272 pp.

Warplanes to Alaska
Blake Smith
ISBN 0-88839-401-2
8.5 x 11 • hc • 256 pp.

Yukon Gold
James/Susan Preyde
ISBN 0-88839-362-8
5.5 x 8.5 • sc • 96 pp.

hancock house

View all HANCOCK HOUSE titles at **www.hancockhouse.com**